211.8 Cimino

Cimino, Richard.

Atheist awakening

ATHEIST AWAKENING

ATHEIST AWAKENING

Secular Activism and Community in America

Richard Cimino and Christopher Smith

OXFORD
UNIVERSITY PRESS

OXFORD
UNIVERSITY PRESS

Oxford University Press is a department of the University of Oxford.
It furthers the University's objective of excellence in research, scholarship,
and education by publishing worldwide.

Oxford   New York
Auckland   Cape Town   Dar es Salaam   Hong Kong   Karachi
Kuala Lumpur   Madrid   Melbourne   Mexico City   Nairobi
New Delhi   Shanghai   Taipei   Toronto

With offices in
Argentina   Austria   Brazil   Chile   Czech Republic   France   Greece
Guatemala   Hungary   Italy   Japan   Poland   Portugal   Singapore
South Korea   Switzerland   Thailand   Turkey   Ukraine   Vietnam

Oxford is a registered trademark of Oxford University Press
in the UK and certain other countries.

Published in the United States of America by
Oxford University Press
198 Madison Avenue, New York, NY 10016

CIP data is on file at the Library of Congress

ISBN 978–0–19–998632–3

1 3 5 7 9 8 6 4 2
Printed in the United States of America
on acid-free paper

Richard Cimino dedicates this book to the
memory of Nancy Cimino.
Christopher Smith dedicates this book to Patricia Johnston

CONTENTS

FOREWORD

Theodore Roosevelt once called patriot Thomas Paine a "filthy little atheist," though, as it was pointed out, Paine was neither filthy nor little—nor an atheist. Still, the term served Roosevelt well in his polemic, for atheists have had a bad reputation in American life. Who are the atheists? Until recently it was rather difficult to find them or define them. Catholic apologist G. K. Chesterton famously observed that when people "choose not to believe in God, they do not thereafter believe in nothing; they then become capable of believing in anything."

Atheists in our culture do not believe in God, but the notion that believing in nothing aptly describes all of them is not true. Those listened to or read by the authors of this book base their beliefs especially around "reason" and "science," however these are described. Or the dissenters against religion may be "humanists," a term signaling that they believe not only in nothing, but also in certain values and human products that demand dedication. Still, most surveyors of this culture observe and chronicle the evidence that "believing in anything," not formal atheism, is the majority alternative to belief in God.

One finds "belief in anything" in what gets called "superstition," "nationalism," "the home team," "the idea of progress," political ideologies, and the countless bazaars that display beckoning options. The presence of so many offerings, especially in parts of the world where people are free to choose what they want to believe, represents an identity problem for many who choose nonbelief in God. How can they engage in what our authors note as "activity and gathering," when many of their programs and beliefs establish their identity as the obverse side of the very religions that usually are coded as agencies for "belief in God"?

Ordinarily, to those for whom belief in God is not a choice, several main alternatives are open. First, they may become apathetic about and indifferent to the claims of religious belief of any sort. Or they may get listed as "nones," a fairly new term for those who simply signal a figurative "none of the above" when a variety of religious choices beckon. Third, they may define themselves as "agnostic," indicating that they do not find compelling reasons to follow a religious vision or belief in God. In all these cases, dedicated atheists often grow frustrated, because agnostics tend to be casual fellow travelers who are not of much use to atheists. They also cannot and do not make the positive contributions to culture that, atheists believe, many of them could be capable of making.

In other words, the nonbelievers need to clarify their thought and live purposefully. The findings in this book concur with other recent studies that find many of them becoming alert. They are undertaking actions apart from and over against believers in God and religious faith in general. The term "awakening" in the book title refers to a specific tradition. It evokes certain historic movements in American and Western European societies, as in the First Great

Awakening in the American colonies in the 1730s. Others, like the Second and Third Great Awakenings, periodically have drawn the attention of chroniclers throughout American history. Such awakenings disturbed the peace of the conventionally religious, who did not welcome what Richard Cimino and Christopher Smith call "surges and incursions." They add up to phenomena that are separate from and that oppose religious belief and what the authors refer to as "activities and gatherings" in its name.

The Awakened—shall we call them that?—face many problems in mixed religious-and-secular cultures. The Awakened recognize that many fellow citizens fear or disdain them and consider them to be subversive of values cherished by the majority. Some—more often than not evangelicals—debate them and fight them in the name of God. They may well be paying compliments to nonbelievers when they picture atheists as having sufficient force to subvert society. Meanwhile, many believers are amused or bemused when they see how many of the features of "organized" atheist culture mimic the religious expressions and communities of believers. Some atheist gatherings look and sound much like the gatherings of God-worshiping believers. Their local associations, new and small though they may be, often seek symbols or ceremonies that show the influence of life in religious congregations, denominations, and voluntary associations. This book introduces readers to many of the forms and expressions of those who choose not to believe in God, or who could not believe if they tried.

When dealing with authors whose books are in process, I like to ask them to finish the sentence, "The thesis of my book is that..." Cimino and Smith, as I read them, appropriately see believers and nonbelievers existing in symbiotic relationships. If the nonbelievers need believers for the fashioning of their own identity, believers often find a need that nonbelievers satisfy.

Both camps find it easier to define their beliefs and their social forms when the other is vital. Whether the Atheist Awakening will result in the formation of a durable opposition to religion is not certain. For now, as the atheists grow more articulate, they and the believers who oppose them both reveal frustration with fellow citizens who occupy what the authors call "no-man's land," and so they try to enlist associates or at least want others to see that much is at stake when citizens "choose to believe in God," in "anything," or in clarified and dedicated "some things" that can make a difference in how people live their lives as individuals or in the larger culture.

Along the way they will "make history" in terms that José Ortega y Gasset spoke of when he noted that "decisive historical changes do not come from great wars, terrible cataclysms, or ingenious inventions." Instead, "It is enough that the [human heart] incline its sensitive crown to one side or the other of the horizon, toward optimism or toward pessimism, toward heroism or toward utility, toward combat or toward peace," and, we might add, "toward belief or unbelief." Cimino and Smith have their eyes on the cultural horizon and are pointing to something "decisive." Their thoughtful and well-documented study will guide us well.

Martin E. Marty is the Fairfax M. Cone Distinguished Service Professor Emeritus at the University of Chicago. He is the author of numerous books on American culture, including *The Infidel: Freethought and American Religion* (Cleveland: World, 1961).

Martin E. Marty

ACKNOWLEDGMENTS

The idea for this book emerged from over a decade of thinking, arguing, researching, and writing about secularist groups and activism.
We would therefore like to thank the people and publications that
supported and encouraged our work in a field that was in its infancy.

We are especially grateful to the Jack Shand Research Grant from
the Society for the Scientific Study of Religion, which provided the
initial support needed to put our project into motion back in 2003.
Much of this initial research was presented at several conferences and
then published in a 2007 article in the journal *Sociology of Religion*.
Chapter 1 in this book draws on several of the concepts and ideas
from this article, even if they have been significantly revised, and we
are indebted to editor David Yamane and reviewers Barry Kosmin
and Frank Pasquale for their constructive criticisms. We were pre-
pared to let things rest on the subject of secularism after this article
until we were invited by Amarnath Amarsingham to contribute a
chapter to his anthology *Religion and the New Atheism* (2010). We
later enlarged on this research for an article on the new atheism in
the *Journal of Religion and Media* in 2011. After input and criticism

by reviewers and other critics at conferences, we further revised this material into what is now chapter 2.

The interesting connection between the new atheism and the new media led us into deeper research on this topic, resulting in a 2012 article in the new journal *Secularism and Nonreligion*. We thank editor Ryan Cragun and reviewers for their criticisms in getting this paper to publication, especially since it helped serve as an early draft for chapter 3 of this book. An earlier version of some of this material is found in our chapter in the book *The Changing World Religion Map*. (2014). We are also grateful to Lori Beaman of the University of Ottawa for the invitation to the 2012 workshop on atheist identities, where some of the ideas on secularist rituals and commemorations were presented and were later to be reworked and expanded upon in chapter 4. An earlier version of this material is in a chapter in the book *Atheist Identities* (2014).

Our thanks also go to Oxford University Press editor Cynthia Read (and her anonymous reviewers) for the criticisms and assistance we needed in turning these scattered efforts into a coherent book. We were glad to find out that Stephen Bullivant was one of our reviewers, and we are grateful for his constructive critique of our work.

From Richard Cimino: The period of writing this book was marked by the passing of my mother, Nancy, and I dedicate this book to her memory—especially since she helped come up with its title! I would also like to thank Michael Cuneo—who gave me the initial feedback and encouragement in researching atheism back in the early 1990s, when it was a real no-man's land for sociologists—and other colleagues, family, and friends for their encouragement and criticism as I formally and informally discussed and presented these findings and ideas over the years. My collaboration with Chris

Smith over the past decade has been the most productive of my career—here's to a great theorist and a good friend.

From Christopher Smith: I would like to dedicate this book to my mother, Patricia Johnston, whose encouragement to think for one's self remains an enduring goal and lasting source of inspiration. For Jane Kelton's support and reassurance—often in times of severe personal doubt—I remain grateful. To Caitlin Maddox: You have made the last few years more than I ever imagined they could be upon returning home. A general shout out to the Smith, Jones, and Johnston families, as well as my many colleagues and professors who have contributed and been supportive in far too many ways to specify here. I would finally like to thank Rich Cimino for extending the hand of friendship and giving the gift of knowing that this work may be read. Last, but far from least, our gratitude goes to the participants and leaders of organized secularist groups who generously shared their time and perspectives with us for well over a decade.

Introduction

When one of the authors first visited a gathering of atheists in the early 1990s, it was a humble affair. A graduate sociology course at Fordham University that the author was taking required a term paper on a religious movement. Since "secular humanism" was a term, or more typically an accusation, that was being thrown around in conspiratorial terms in some Christian circles, it seemed like a good candidate for closer study. The small group of about ten mainly elderly white men that met in a drafty basement of an old Universalist church on Manhattan's Upper West Side didn't seem like a threat to anyone. In fact, the proceedings had a besieged tone, with members complaining that they were under threat by the growing influence of the religious right.

Dennis, a banker who had recently joined the society, said atheism and secular humanism were a hard sell among the younger generations. "Secular humanism appeals to intellectuals, but kids today want to earn money.... They ignore things that don't meet an immediate need." He added, with some frustration, "I'm thirty-nine, and I'm often the youngest person in secular humanist meetings.... There are not many women also. I'm having a hard time finding a wife who is a secular humanist."

Fast-forward twenty years: On a rainy Saturday in April, a throng of over ten thousand atheists and secular humanists filled the

National Mall in Washington for the Reason Rally. Some organizers of the event estimated twenty thousand participants. Numbers were a serious business to these atheists; the aim of the rally was to demonstrate to the rest of America that the nonreligious had enough clout not to be threatened politically or socially. Just ten years earlier, a similar event was staged in the same place; it drew only twenty-five hundred and was marked by considerable disunity among the various secularist groups. In 2012, secularists were united enough to bring the major groups together, and a brief survey of the crowd revealed that their members were just as likely to be young men and women sporting tattoos and T-shirts with atheist slogans as the stereotypical middle-aged and elderly white males (also T-shirted). Running the logistics for most of the event were energetic members of the Secular Student Alliance, an organization that grew from 125 atheist student groups across the United States in 2009 to 395 affiliates in 2013. Of those 395 affiliates, 80 percent have a Facebook group with an average of 97 members, which combined totals 28,256. In 2009, when we initially contacted the organization, they published a newsletter with roughly 4,000 subscribers nationwide.

What had happened between 1992 and 2012? Had hordes of churchgoing Americans thrown off their faiths to embrace a lack of faith with a religious fervor—a third Great Awakening, as our title may suggest? A sober examination of the rate of nonbelievers does not show a dramatic increase of atheists over the past two decades. Not so coincidentally, some growth has occurred of those claiming a disbelief in God, along with a much larger increase of religious nonaffiliation, especially among the younger generations (Pew Research Center 2012). Yet the percentage does not reflect the swelling atheist presence and activism we have witnessed in the last decade. In this book we argue that there has been an *awakening* of atheist identity and politics largely among those who were already nonreligious. *Something* happened in American society in the last three decades that mobilized nonbelievers into action, and we believe that something is the increasing public—often political—presence of religion.

The practice of revealing oneself—coming out—as an atheist has never been a matter of treading a well-worn path in the United States; instead, claiming an atheist identity can still carry a significant stigma. Public opinion polls continue to confirm the prevalence of old stereotypes that brand atheists as immoral, un-American, and often angry. The state of Arkansas has a constitutional provision disqualifying atheists from holding public office or testifying in court.

The growth of conservative and often political religion has not only "raised the consciousnesses" of individual atheists but also compelled secularist (our term for atheist and other nonreligious) organizations to retool their strategies to wage both a defensive and offensive battle against their ideological and political antagonists. Whereas atheism was once largely an apolitical stance that usually only implied a position of strict separation of church and state, this diffuse movement has been politicized to a similar extent to that of conservative Christians. Where four decades ago, it would not be clear whether a professing atheist would necessarily be a Republican or Democrat, today that guessing game is largely over. This pattern is reflected in the reality that the Democratic Party is increasingly the home of the nonaffiliated (or "nones"), while the Republicans have become the party of conservative religionists. Moreover, committed atheists who participate in secularist organizations are far more likely to support gay marriage, be pro-choice, and support government intervention when it comes to the economy (Williamson and Yancey 2013), which could open up the possibility of a gay-atheist alliance within the Democratic Party, given their overlapping opposition to conservative religion, even as they distance themselves from many of the postmodern theoretical/intellectual resources that gays have used in their struggles (Taira 2012). Nonetheless, all the current research on the political affiliation of secularists seems to point to them falling predominantly left of center, especially on social issues. Another study from 2010, published in the secular humanist magazine *Free Inquiry* surveying its subscribers/readers, for example, found that 75 percent self-described as liberal, progressive, or socialist (Flynn 2012a). In our surveys we found similar numbers, although we also had some strong stirrings toward libertarianism and fiscal conservatism that could potentially draw some toward independent candidates and away from the Democratic Party in the future. Of course, given the trends, the candidate would likely need to take a firmly and public antireligion stance and end things like tax breaks for churches and other faith-based initiatives, which Democrats have continued to support and keep in place.

In this book, however, we take the focus off the culture wars that journalists and sociologists have documented so well to look at a significant movement within the "progressive" side of this enduring conflict in American society. While political identity and behavior form an important part of American secularism, it is not the whole story. As sociologists, we want to look at how atheists are forming a collective identity and building a community as well as engaging in activism. Throughout this book we discuss the role of social media in allowing atheists to connect and discover one another as part of a virtual community of like-minded strangers. A big part of this phenomenon involves atheists decoupling themselves from other roles, obligations, and identities and coming out with their atheism as their primary identity. Increasingly, secularists have identified themselves with other minorities in America, even borrowing from the gay rights movement as they seek to come out of the closet and claim an atheist identity among their families, friends, and the public in general. In using the metaphor of the closet, nonbelievers are obviously attempting to draw a parallel to the gay rights movement. Richard Dawkins, in an interview on CNN, confirms this comparison: "I think we're in the same position the gay movement was in a few decades ago. There was a need for people to come out. The more people came out, the more people had the courage to come out. I think that's the case with atheists. [We] are more numerous than anybody realizes" (Hooper 2006).

The fact that we are examining secularist organizations rather than atheist intellectuals during a period when the new atheism has received wide attention due to the best-selling books by such figures associated with the phenomenon as Dawkins, Christopher Hitchens, and Sam Harris, marks our work as unique. Most treatments of atheism have looked more at how individuals develop an atheist identity or lose their former faiths than at the organizational dynamics driving secularist groups. We pay attention to the new atheism, but we attempt to understand the phenomenon in terms of atheism as a social movement with a particular complexion in the context of the United States (despite its largely British origins). Proponents and critics both admit that the new atheism was largely generated and propelled by the media—both new and old—so we think it is important to explain how the media environment of America in the midst of globalization fits in with the particular "socio-logic" of secularism, allowing it to expand and create a new kind of community. This especially applies to social media and the Internet, which allow secularists to speak out, reach out, and connect as atheists, thereby creating a new kind of collective identity that bypasses previous means of community-building in a particular locale (although it does this, too) while also mobilizing highly individualistic freethinkers into various forms of activism.

At the same time, no community or movement is complete without its rituals, special experiences, and collective emotions serving as the glue that holds them together. In the case of atheists, capturing the affective quality of nonreligion is a challenge not only because of the aforementioned individualism, but also because atheists by definition reject religion and its building blocks of rituals and spirituality. We found, however, that the matter is not so cut-and-dried; in fact, atheists and various kinds of humanists are clashing among themselves over the need for rites of passage and even something called "secular spirituality."

The individualism driving organized secularism offers a place for schisms, subgroups, and conflicts to flourish. For the purpose of identifying and analyzing common trends we categorize the various nonreligion groups under the broad heading of "secularists," though the participants themselves go by an array of names ranging from freethinkers to secular humanists to religious humanists and "brights." Behind each self-identification are different and even clashing histories, traditions, and ways of being an atheist.

Atheists have been around as long as religions (Stark and Finke 2000). But only in the last two centuries have nontheists begun to organize for discussion, debate, fellowship, and activism. Organized "free-thought" and atheism emerged in the eighteenth century, with Thomas Paine's book *Age of Reason* and other antireligious tracts of the times playing an important role in spreading and popularizing such views. These early secularists began by questioning orthodox Christian doctrines, but eventually they came to be critical of all forms of religion. Like today, such freethinkers or rationalists were highly individualistic, but they gathered around societies (such as the Infidel Society) and periodicals, which in some cases were modeled after churches (Campbell 1972). Until recently, secularist organizations struggled in drawing support and participation and were often at cross-purposes with each other. Such figures as Madalyn Murray O'Hair drew wide publicity and controversy to the atheist cause as they sought to counteract the influence of religion in public and political life. The controversy often accompanies the politics— an issue that secularists still struggle with, given the stigma that accompanies nonbelief and the mere mention of "atheist" in some parts of the United States. Debate persists about whether using the term "atheist" is appropriate when attempting to gain political traction, even as research suggests that antiatheist bias is apparent whether the term "atheist" is used or not. Another strain of secularism sought closer connections to traditional forms of religion—an issue that continues to divide atheists and humanists (a point we discuss at greater length in the following chapters). Essentially, secularists embracing "religious humanism"—defining "religious" in a functional rather than substantive way—can be traced back to the Unitarian and Universalist movements that emerged after a segment of churches in the eighteenth century rejected such Christian doctrines. Both of these groups grew increasingly liberal in later periods as they discarded other supernatural elements of Christianity. A segment of Unitarian-Universalism and similar groups that formed in the twentieth century—such as Ethical Culture, the American Humanist Association, and Humanistic Judaism—have held on to a religious identity, claiming a tax exemption for their congregations, creating seminaries, and, in some cases, ordaining their leaders, as well as holding rites of passage for their members. In contrast, secular humanism, which broke off from religious humanism in the 1970s, challenged the need for any religious baggage (although, again, as we discuss in depth in chapter 4, even hard-core atheists are debating the use of rituals). While atheists may make up about 3 to 4 percent of the U.S. population (and about 30 percent of the nonaffiliated population), the percentage of such

Americans who are involved in secularist organizations is far smaller (Hout and Fischer 2002; Funk et al. 2012). One recent study found an estimated 3,109 secularist groups of various types (Garcia and Blankholm 2013). But as we note above, the number of active atheists has obviously grown in the last twenty years. Of course, being an "active" atheist is not the same thing as being an active Christian or Muslim. Many may not attend weekly atheist or humanist meetings, or even belong to national secularist organizations. By "active atheists" we mean those who identify with the atheist cause and participate in some form of fellowship and activism, whether virtual or actual. In any event, we call this new atheist consciousness an "awakening" in that a confluence of cultural, political, and internal secularist group dynamics have come together to create a perfect storm of atheist vitality, similar in many ways to religious vitality (actually, we derived the title "Atheist Awakening" during the aforementioned Reason Rally, where one of the speakers compared the gathering to the Great Awakening in American religious history).

Most books on atheism have addressed the subject either apologetically, like the new atheist books, or polemically, as seen in the scores of works defending theism. Our book looks at the subject through a sociological perspective that seeks to avoid bias in either direction. Although our approach to organized secularism is unique, it is part of a renewed interest in atheism as reflected in several scholarly and popular works that have been published recently. Aside from works of philosophy and theology (from atheist and theist perspectives), other books on atheism have either been historical or based on secularism on societal and individual levels, while largely bypassing its organizational aspects (Jacoby 2004; Zuckerman 2011). The scholarly treatment of secularism (Taylor 2007; Asad 2003) has looked at it as a social force and a theological and philosophical issue with considerable sophistication. Yet such works have not focused on secularity as an intentional and organized movement with its own identity and strategies for creating a more secular America and defending its interests. Other recent studies have looked at the psychological and demographic characteristics of atheists (Bainbridge 2005; Galen 2009; Beit-Hallahmi 2007; Martin 2002; Hunsberger and Altermeyer 2006), but they do not examine closely the collective expressions of atheism and secularism. However, the sociological dimensions of secularity have come under new scrutiny with recent publications in the burgeoning field of secular studies, which have greatly helped our own research and analysis; may their tribe increase (e.g., see Amarasingam 2010; Kosmin and Keysar 2007; LeDrew 2013; Zuckerman 2010; Smith 2011, 2013).

For this book we interviewed fifty-two self-identified atheists, undertook participant observation of eighteen special events and meetings, and conducted online surveys of three hundred and seventeen atheists and humanists connected to local and national secularist organizations. We also conducted textual analysis of *Free Inquiry*, the magazine of the Council for Secular Humanism; the *American Atheist*, the magazine of the American Atheists; and about 150 websites, blogs, and other social media issued by secularists of various strains (see the appendix for more details on our methods). While we cannot claim that our methods are statistically representative of American atheists and humanists, we do believe our research illuminates a significant dimension of the broad secularist movement. Throughout this book we have attempted to reflect the diversity of the broad secularist movement in the United States, even if much of our data is drawn from research of secular humanism and organized atheism—the two largest and most prominent streams of secularism today.

HOW THE BOOK IS ORGANIZED

In chapter 1, we present the premise that runs through most of this book: understanding the secularist awakening is difficult apart from America's unique religious character and the influence it has on secularism in all its varied definitions, understandings, and social forms. The organized atheist and secular humanist movements have long operated under the presumption of secularism progressing and inevitably overtaking religious influence in American society. In the last two decades, however, progressive secularism has come under increasing criticism. We examine how atheists and secular humanists—as social actors "making history" under conditions they themselves have not chosen—have responded to the complications and difficulties of secularism becoming a dominant force in the United States; we also consider how they have rethought their role and strategy from that of acting as the secular vanguard to assuming a subcultural identity and engaging in defensive competition in order to find a place in American society. Briefly, they have done so by adopting such strategies as creating a niche for secular humanism among the unchurched and secular seekers; mimicking and adapting various aspects of evangelicalism, even as they target this movement as their main antagonist; and making use of minority discourse and identity politics. In pursuing such identity politics we see the tension at work between what Manuel Castells (1997) refers to as an oppositional or *resistance identity*—and a *project identity*—assumed "when social actors, on the basis of whichever cultural materials are available to them, build a new identity that redefines their position in society and, by so doing, seek the transformation of [the] overall social structure" (8). Whereas the former is firmly entrenched as a subcultural identity, we might say that the latter is a subculture looking to challenge such a status (on the basis of that very status). The defensive posture of claiming minority status, which we highlight in chapter 1, stands in sharp contrast to the positive and triumphant statements of the inevitable victory of secularism that atheists and humanists expressed in the twentieth century. Remember, however, that the way one takes pride in one's own identity group is rarely the way one appeals to outsiders. This also helps one to understand the contrast between a more extreme stance based on a critique of religion in all its forms and a more moderate stance based around commonalities and the desire to just be accepted, or to change prejudice. The two strategies coexist, but they can also cause tensions between the various secularist subgroups.

We look in chapter 2 at how atheist and secular humanist organizations have interpreted and appropriated the new atheist phenomenon. Just about the time that secularists were coming to terms with a subcultural identity, somewhat suddenly and unexpectedly they found themselves in the middle of an atheist revival. Admittedly the revival was literary, conspired by major publishers and authors already quite active in the secularist movement, but the books and the surrounding publicity created a new attention space for atheist books as well as atheists themselves. We argue that a connection exists between new atheism as a broad social phenomenon and the publicly emerging needs and desires of atheists and secularists; they are both cause and effect of one another.

In the background of this revitalization is the confluence of the new atheist literature, on the one hand, and an uptake in the use of social media, on the other. These books—as bestsellers—are the cultural content most readily available to be conveyed through these networks. In terms of secularist culture, the extension and transformation of communicative networks, the growing market for atheist books, and the public emergence of atheists as a social group are all reciprocally influential. While critics and even some secularists claim the new atheists are doing more harm than good, we argue that such critiques ultimately miss the function of the books: taken collectively they provide a highly diverse population of secularists with a common and general set of issues and ideas in which to imagine a sense of community, even as many within the milieu are critical of the authors and particular arguments or aspects of their works.

A significant expansion of websites and blogs dealing with atheism has occurred in the last decade, opening up active spaces for atheists to construct and share mutual concerns about their situation at a time when American public life is still largely functioning under a norm of religiosity in many communities and institutional contexts (Cimino and Smith 2007, 2011).

Building on the previous one, in chapter 3 we focus more closely on the role of the Internet in the formation of an atheist collective identity. In discussing an atheist collective identity, we are referring to diverse groups—ranging from hard-core atheists to agnostics, brights, and various kinds of humanists. Premised on a model of narrowcasting against a backdrop of broadcasting, the Internet reveals this plurality of smaller identity groupings within a larger, general, and increasingly global secularist collective that is informationally greater than the sum of its individual participants. Using textual analysis of secularist websites, we analyze some of the expressive forms of atheist cyberactivism and how this electronic medium has facilitated a more visible and active secular identity, which we consider a form of activism in terms of promoting the importance of secularist concerns and issues in public discourse. Just as feminists and the LGBT community have focused on creating public, political identities from their varied and different concerns, atheists are bringing their varied expressions of nonbelief and atheist concerns into the public sphere as well. In the second part we seek to situate this atheist activism in a larger political context and explore the potential for atheists to move beyond discourse and institutionalize the symbolic power expressed online. Drawing on social movement theory, we conclude with a brief look at gains made and obstacles that remain.

In a reaction to the new atheism, a segment of secularists have been advocating a more positive atheism that seeks to cooperate with religions to some extent, but even those maintaining a polemical stance are wrestling with the need to provide a sense of community and rites of passage for newcomers and the next generations. In chapter 4 we look at how organized secularist groups have sought to create nontheist alternatives to traditional religion—offering, for example, atheist assemblies or services, funerals, weddings, meditation services, or commemorations of "secular saints" such as Charles Darwin. Even the antireligious polemics and humor presented at secularist rallies and meetings can be viewed as rituals. Through the ethnographic method we examine specific secular rituals organized by secular humanist groups, but we also conducted an Internet survey and content analysis of atheists and atheist publications about the need for a positive atheism and secular rituals. We found that some secularists even talk of a "secular spirituality," while others take a more cerebral, rationalist approach. We argue that these secular alternatives, including antireligious humor, provide atheists and secular humanists with rituals of solidarity, creating a strong collective identity and a sense of community. Other rituals and commemorations provide legitimization, as they seek nonpartisan outreach to, and links with, wider nonsecularist society.

In the conclusion we examine the prospects of secularism and its interaction with religion in the United States. We discuss how secularism is related to secularization. Whereas one is an intentional movement to bring about a more nonreligious American society, the other is a gradual sociological process involving not only individuals becoming less religious but also institutions and spheres of society gaining autonomy from religious authority. It can be argued that the United States has to a large extent experienced the latter kind of secularization in much of its history, but not the former. While avoiding making many predictions about the future of secularism in the United States, we next look at the prospects of secularism in America, in terms of its institutional barriers and opportunities as well as a cultural force. Finally, we discuss the possibilities of religious-secularist dialogue.

We have approached this book as interested observers-scholars. Neither of us are card-carrying members of, or are even involved in, secularist movements or organizations. We came to this subject as sociology students at the New School for Social Research in New York and found that it touched on a number of areas in which we were interested—secularism and secularization, social movements, and the sociology of the media—and decided to collaborate in research and writing, leading to several coauthored articles and book chapters. While these publications and research helped us create a framework for writing this book, we should note that this work is largely originally written, based on new and updated research. While complete objectivity is impossible, we have tried to be as unbiased as possible in researching and writing about the groups and individuals involved in organized secularism. If readers find any shortcomings in this regard, at least we have striven to be fair. Our respective locations in Oklahoma and New York have helped us avoid parochial perspectives, providing countless examples about how regional context is central in ascertaining the scope and influence of secularism (both the organized and unorganized varieties) and religiosity in the United States.

A sociologist friend used to say that he was not so much concerned about being interesting as "being interested." That the personalities, groups, and movements of organized secularism have kept both of us interested in this topic for well over a decade is no small matter. We hope that such fascination and interest rub off on readers as well.

Chapter 1

Organized Secularism Beyond the "Humanist Twenty-First Century"

Oblivious to the main speaker at the podium, a crowd gathered at the edge of Washington's National Mall during the 2012 Reason Rally, most likely the largest atheist gathering in American history. A large circle of atheists surrounded a Christian protestor as they engaged in a shouting match over the finer points of Christian sexual morality. In the back-and-forth on arcane philosophical points that ensued, both parties seemed to be thoroughly enjoying themselves. The sight of atheists and Christians locked in contention was not uncommon at the public atheist events (and in online interactions) we have observed over the past decade.

It all brought to mind G. K. Chesterton's novel *The Ball and the Cross*, which tells the whimsical story of a fiery atheist editor and a devout Catholic debating and dueling throughout England. In their public skirmishes about the existence of God, miracles, and the value of rationalism, the combatants encounter more puzzlement and amusement than sympathy from onlookers, while officials merely seek to have them committed. As they battle on, the pair realizes that they share more in common with each other than with the indifferent masses surrounding them. At one point, the atheist editor proclaims, "This man and I are alone in the modern world in that we think that God is essentially important. I think He does not exist; that is where the importance comes in for me" (Chesterton 1963: 76).

Like the dueling duo in Chesterton's story, today's atheist and Christian in a sense need each other. The nominally religious and the "spiritual but not religious" crowd may view atheist polemics as being irrelevant or in bad taste, but the atheist critique is not really aimed in such directions in the first place. Through provocation and trying to debunk their religious antagonists, atheism gains traction in society and develops a public identity. In fact, the contentious nature of atheism is an important factor in its new visibility and organizational growth.

Atheists have always been a minority in American society— and not a very popular one. Surveys consistently show public disapproval of atheism and atheists. But even in the midst of popular opposition, atheists and other "free thinkers" have thought they were on the verge of a secularist "great awakening" in America—a term used frequently at the Reason Rally in Washington. Just as evangelical Protestants up until one hundred years ago held a largely optimistic view of the future and the end times (known as postmillennialism), secular humanists and atheists also expected that a progressive, secular "kingdom" would emerge as societies threw off a primitive theistic mindset and matured into educated adulthood.

As historian Sidney Warren (1966: 231) writes of these movements in the eighteenth and nineteenth centuries, "Freethinkers never doubted the correctness of their position, for they viewed history as a continuous struggle between the forces of light and darkness. They were, they felt, carrying the torch of reason in an otherwise religious world of bigotry and superstition." As secular rationalism gained ascendancy in many American institutions in the late nineteenth and early twentieth centuries, the expectation

of a comprehensive secular revolution was widely shared by organized humanist and atheist leaders and thinkers, as well as by scientists and educational leaders (Smith 2003). This "progressive
secularism," understood as the dominance of naturalistic and scientific thought over supernatural explanations of reality, was seen
as America's future. That widespread secularism has not been established in the United States, and many social scientists now question
such a scenario for the future (Berger 1999; Stark and Finke 2000),
has become an overriding concern for secularist movements. In
this chapter, we will look at how secularism is coexisting and often
thriving in a religious, if pluralistic, society. But in doing so, secularists are engaging in a change of strategy and self-understanding.
Nowhere is this clearer than in the organizational life of contemporary American atheism and secular humanism, which is a movement blending atheism with a positive system of ethics.

SECULAR HUMANISM, ATHEISM, AND RELIGIOUS ROOTS

The complex relationship between secularism and religious America
can be illustrated in the way secular humanism has gradually disas-
sociated itself from any ties and connotations with organized religion. The religious roots of humanism can be found in Unitarian
and Universalist churches, which developed after a segment of
Congregational churches in the eighteenth century rejected key
Christian doctrines such as the Trinity and the teaching that God
can condemn people to hell. Unitarian-Universalism grew increasingly liberal in later periods as it questioned other traditional beliefs,
including theism. In 1933 the *Humanist Manifesto* was issued largely
by Unitarians, calling for a world community based on secular and

liberal values. The fledgling movement based around this manifesto was called "religious humanism" (*Humanist Manifesto*; Walter 1998).

Although the use of the term "religious" was meant to stress profound human experiences and activities while excluding any supernatural beliefs and explanations of reality, some religious humanist leaders and participants objected to any uses of religion. Thus, in an effort to emphasize its secular identity and credentials, the authors of the *Humanist Manifesto II* (1973) removed any reference to religious humanism. In fact, the document asserted that while some humanists may prefer the religious label, such redefinitions of religion "often perpetuate old dependencies and escapisms." The dilemma about whether to accept a religious or secular framework was the main factor in a schism within the primary humanist group, the American Humanist Association (AHA), in the late 1970s. The conflict resulted in the birth of the Council for Democratic and Secular Humanism in 1980, later renamed the Council for Secular Humanism. Thus, while religious humanists claim that humanism is a nontheistic religion, secular humanists define their movement as a strictly secular philosophy and value system and eschew any religious language.

In its three decades, the council has been instrumental in changing the contours of organized secularism in the United States. One way of organizing secularists to form congregations (in some cases holding churchlike services) was largely viewed as a failure in maintaining and expanding the movement. There have also been alternatives, such as forming clublike associations in clear disassociation from religious congregations (Campbell 1972). The association model is still present among many humanist and atheist groups, although the council has stressed international outreach to elites, particularly targeting opinion leaders and the media and entertainment worlds. The council's sole original goal of publishing its magazine *Free Inquiry* was broadened to include an effort to strengthen a sense of community among secular humanists and extend its message to other secular and skeptical Americans seeking support and resources. During the 1990s, specialized humanist groups were formed, such as African-Americans for Humanism and Secular Organizations for Sobriety (which serves as a secular alternative to Alcoholics Anonymous and other addiction programs). In 1996 the council founded the Campus Freethought Alliance, now called the Secular Student Alliance, which has grown rapidly, enlisting students and faculty in over 350 universities, colleges, and high schools around the country. Secular student groups have formed in the Bible Belt, giving atheist and secular humanist students a support system in the face of overwhelming conservative Christian involvement on campus. Debates and even cooperation on joint programs are held with Christian groups on these campuses. These groups have also sprouted up in less expected places, such as Ivy League schools, where intellectual trends such as postmodernism have galvanized secularist students who criticize what they see as the decreasing emphasis on reason in academia. The focus on outreach is also evident in the formation of Centers for Inquiry (CFI), which are educational and outreach centers that coordinate secular humanist and skeptical activity in a given region. CFIs in New York and Los Angeles, for instance, target the media and entertainment worlds with a secular humanist message. There are a reported fifteen Centers for Inquiry throughout the world, and 876 groups affiliated with the centers (including approximately 120 local secular humanist groups in the United States).

Distinct from the secular humanist movement, the atheist movement traces its roots to the "freethought," antireligious societies that developed in nineteenth-century America. The larger groups today are the American Atheists, which has approximately four thousand members, and the Freedom from Religion Foundation, which has experienced significant growth, increasing from five thousand to more than nineteen thousand members in 2013 (although membership does not necessarily mean active participation in activities) (Winston 2013). In recent years, several other atheist groups and websites have been founded, ranging from the "Brights" to the Richard Dawkins Foundation. Organized atheists have been among the strongest activists for nontheism, often challenging religious actions and groups in court. Humanists frequently contrast their positive approach (stressing the creation of a world community and defending human rights) with the more reactionary and hard-line stance that atheists take in defending and promoting nontheism. Atheists claim that secular humanists have diluted the antitheistic message by adding philosophical and ethical teachings to their agenda.

CREATING THE SECULARIST SUBCULTURE

Sociologists and secularists themselves both show an abiding interest in the numbers of atheists and secular humanists in the United States. As we discussed in the Introduction, most surveys show a significant increase in the number of Americans identifying as nonaffiliated (Keysar et al. 2003), although it is still not clear what percentage of these "nones" are atheist or agnostic. Secularists see the growth of the unaffiliated as a potential windfall for the movement, in a similar way that Christians claim the unchurched as potential converts ripe for the harvest. The use (and misuse) of numbers by secularists provides a helpful window into understanding how secularists create a place for themselves in American society. The religious economy theory of Stark and Finke (2000: 209) holds that a persistent minority in society will reject organized religion, but that this segment of nonbelievers may be too small and weak to create a distinct niche for secularism. Under what conditions, though, might that niche develop? Christian Smith's (1998) subcultural identity theory argues that maintaining a tension with society can strengthen the particular beliefs and practices of a group, regardless of its size. In fact, as with the evangelicals Smith studied, secular humanists and atheists have assumed a position in American society that stresses maintaining boundaries and reinforcing group identity in the face of a larger external threat. In other words, secular humanists and atheists feel "embattled" in a persistently religious society. Just as Smith found that evangelicals thrived as a subculture through their sense of embattlement, we argue that secularists have found a similar level of vitality. This identity formation is linked to secularist social, political, and cultural gains and should not be conceived solely in reactionary and defensive terms.

We argue that the actions and interactions of atheist and secular humanist groups and leaders—even among those holding to a strongly secularist view of the future—reveal how they have internalized both their minority status and the failure of progressive secularism to take hold in the United States, which is evident in the three strategies they pursue in their attempts to not only survive but grow in a largely religious society. First, they are competing and positioning themselves to attract "secular seekers," who are similar to spiritual seekers or "questers" in their persistent search for authentic communities of meaning while remaining highly individualistic (Roof 1999). Second, they have borrowed elements from their main antagonists—evangelical Protestants—in defining themselves and rallying others to their cause. Third, they have taken up minority discourse and identity politics in pressing for group rights and equal treatment in society.

Optimism about the eventual victory of secularism has historically been the rule rather than the exception in organized secularist movements. Philosopher Corliss Lamont (1990), often considered the father of modern secular humanism, fully expected that organized religion would continue to decline into irrelevance and obscurity late in the twentieth century. The aforementioned *Humanist Manifesto* of 1933 and the *Humanist Manifesto II* of 1973—considered to be the charters of the organized humanist movement in the United States—both viewed secularism as ascending. *Humanist Manifesto II* predicted that the twenty-first century would be the "humanist century," as new strides in morals, ethics, and technology replaced older religious systems. Such changes as greater availability of birth control, abortion, and divorce were thought to signal a social revolution that would overturn religious values. Some secularist leaders still assert certainty about the eventual progress of secularism. As Ellen Johnson, a past president of American Atheists, said during an interview, "Religion is on the wane. That's why there is government support [for it]. That's why it's going to the schools . . . and to Capitol Hill. Today religion is being bailed out by the government. That's why religion is equated with patriotism."

With far less optimism, the drafters of an updated *Humanist Manifesto 2000* (1999: 6) stated that "the world is now divided, as fundamentalisms have rekindled, contesting the principles of humanism and secularism and demanding a return to the religiosity of a premodern era." Yet there is a far from monolithic response among secularists concerning the influence of religion in America. Some leaders have repudiated their earlier optimism about the future dominance of secularism, while others have held on to this optimistic vision, believing that the United States will eventually follow Europe into a more secular mode of living. The popularity of the "new atheism," at least in book sales, though not necessarily in converting people to atheism, has sought to revive the conviction that societal secularization is just around the corner. But up until 2008, there was clearly a loss of confidence among secular humanist leaders regarding the victory of secularism, at least in American society. For example, the summer 2002 issue of *Free Inquiry* magazine, with the cover story "Anywhere but Here," laments how the United States stands as an exception to the way "the developed world is becoming more secular." Acknowledging the attraction of religions, Paul Kurtz, the late leader and founder of the Council for Secular Humanism, suggested that they "will continue with us in the foreseeable future and will not easily wither away," since, for the "bulk of humankind," religion presents "moral poetry, aesthetic inspiration, reformative ceremonial rituals, which act out and dramatize the human condition and . . . seek to slake the thirst for meaning and purpose" (Kurtz 2002).

In our interviews among participants in the secular humanist movement, we found many who viewed themselves as an embattled minority with an uncertain future in religious America. Alan, a thirty-five-year-old secular humanist interviewed in Tulsa, neatly summed up this line of thought: "Don't you know Oral Roberts is over here [by] one mile? So, we are talking in the shadow of the prayer tower. . . . I think there will always be a small group of people, like us, who will be critical thinkers and who will reject the dogma that's handed to us from the time we are children. I think the masses will continue [in religion]." In New York, there was the same positioning with regard to the religious drift of the greater society. Barbara, a seventy-year-old member of a Long Island secular humanist group, said she has given up hope of convincing "those who believe the whole kit and caboodle of religion. You really can't argue with them. We have [to realize] we live in a theistic world."

There was a change of tone about the prospects of progressive secularism after 2008. Part of the reason for the greater confidence was the influence of the new atheism, represented by a spate of best-selling atheist books, a subject we address further in chapter 2. But the election of Barack Obama and the perceived failure of the religious right buoyed up expectations of a more secular society, especially after the new president promised to represent unbelievers as well as believers. Yet the theme of struggle and the fear of a reversal into religious superstition has remained a central line of discourse among secularist leaders as well as laypeople. They are still trying to negotiate a world that seems to be beyond progressive secularism, and where religion has assumed an increasingly public role.

The loss of certainty about the progress of secularism in American society among secular humanists and atheists has driven them in the direction of seeking new forms of community and support. In his attempt to map out the moral and religious terrain of baby boomers, Wade Clark Roof (1999) points to four broad groupings: questers or spiritual seekers, born-again Christians, dogmatists, and secularists. While many of the core members of secular humanist and atheist groups remain older, a clear growth of younger generations has occurred in these organizations, especially in the Bible Belt regions of the U.S. South. Roof notes that those baby boomers most influenced by the changes and revolutions of the 1960s, emphasizing personal autonomy and the questioning of traditional authority and norms, are the most secular of their peers. David, a forty-eight-year-old secular humanist from New York, stated in an interview that he was "very into sixties culture. The most progressive ideas in the sixties didn't come from religious people.... The Kennedy administration... the social activists, all of the compassion of that time did not come from religious people. The religious people back then were the ones saying 'pull yourself up by your own bootstraps.' The ascent of faith-based social policies today is just the escalation of those cruel policies."

Like their questing counterparts, secularists express a desire for a community that allows for personal exploration, independent of traditional authority, and that also offers a place in which to raise and educate their children. This interest often leads to involvement in organized groups. Many of our interviewees underwent a gradual process of finding and constructing an atheist or secular humanist identity, often including involvement in various humanist and liberal religious groups. Becoming involved in secular humanism was for many a way of claiming a positive identity, whereas claiming the atheist label was often viewed as just being against religion. For their part, atheists often criticized self-identifying secular humanists for discarding the atheist label in order to avoid controversy and derision in society. Jonathan, a forty-seven-year-old musician and real estate broker in New York, was brought up in a nominally Jewish home but never considered himself to be religious. When he got married, he tried attending a Reform Jewish temple with his wife, a Catholic. "My wife wanted to have some religion, and she didn't care what it was. Judaism seemed less problematic. It's less of a faith-based perspective, less about being redeemed and all that other stuff." They went through classes at the synagogue, but he grew dissatisfied. "Even that disgusted me. There was no way I could do it. I'd be a hypocrite. I think everyone believed it because they [thought] everyone else was believing it." But with the birth of his daughter, Jonathan realized that he needed a "community that represents something I believe in." By that time he had developed a nonjudgmental belief system based on his idea that, owing to genetics, people do not have free will and are not responsible for their actions, and that judging others is therefore impossible. Through the Internet he still was looking for some group or community in which to raise his child. Although secular humanism carried a strong belief in free will, he found this belief system closest to his own and began to participate in secular humanist activities in the New York area.

Many of those we interviewed made the transition from religious beliefs to secular humanism with a stopover at a Unitarian-Universalist or a liberal Protestant congregation. Since Unitarianism is the main seedbed of much of the humanist move-ment, it is no surprise that many secular humanists have had contact with this religion. The turn away from Unitarianism is, for some, partial or gradual, as some still rely on the denomination to pro-vide rites of passage such as weddings and funerals—services that other religious humanist groups, such as Ethical Culture, also offer. Unitarian-Universalism's larger membership and more stable struc-tures, as well as the institutional weight it can exert on social issues, are appealing in places where conservative Christianity predomi-nates. The large Unitarian church in Oklahoma draws members of a smaller secular humanist group to its services and other activi-ties, even though the minister is not a secular humanist. As James, a member of the secular humanist group in Tulsa, said, "Lately, I'm embarrassed to say that I've been hanging out with the Unitarians. It's, I hate to say, more fun. I go there. I listen to the sermon, which is usually about morality. Sometimes [the minister] hits it from a spiritual angle, but I really enjoy the sermons." The fact that there are more women at the Unitarian church than in the humanist meeting also particularly appeals to this single man.

Still, a growing trend toward Christian or alternative forms of spirituality and away from nontheism in Unitarian-Universalism has tended to alienate secular humanists from what was once their strongest ally, although there is an association of humanists within the denomination (Dart 2001). Roger, a sixty-five-year-old teacher, followed a familiar path of secular seeking. Raised Catholic, he adopted an atheist stance through reading philosophy, including the works of Ayn Rand. He was introduced to Ethical Culture and then moved on to Unitarianism. Since then, as Unitarians have moved to more religious and spiritual teachings, he has distanced himself from the church, joining the American Humanist Association (AHA) and becoming a "chaplain" with that group. As a chaplain he organizes discussions, does counseling, and participates in interfaith events representing the AHA. Roger values his involvement in the secular humanist group for providing a sense of community. "I love going to a place where I can speak my mind, where I can say I'm an atheist easily." He still seeks an alliance with the humanist wing of Unitarian-Universalism (the church has humanist, Christian, pagan, and other associations within its structure). To his distress, he finds that younger, more religious members of the AHA are using the language of spirituality. The few attempts to create a coalition between these various groups of freethinkers have failed. He sees more promise in promoting ties with liberal religious groups to fight the influence of the religious right.

Secular humanist competition with other freethought groups is evident in its claim that it represents the largest and fastest-growing segment of the broader movement. The Council for Secular Humanism's outreach strategy has shown a measure of success. Its magazine *Free Inquiry* has twenty-seven thousand subscribers, and *Skeptical Inquirer* has thirty-five thousand subscribers, according to its government-required circulation statements, a higher circulation figure than any other freethought publication. There is likely some readership overlap between the two magazines, particularly since the *Skeptical Inquirer* has moved beyond debunking paranormal phenomena to include critical treatment of new and traditional religions. The competitive thrust is evident in the way council officials repeatedly refuse to disclose associate membership figures and instead often cite a much higher circulation of one hundred thousand for *Free Inquiry* and the *Skeptical Inquirer* as the most accurate indicator of its strength (it is equally difficult to obtain membership figures from American Atheists and the newer organizations). The readership estimates of magazines are admittedly a weak measure of the vitality of a social movement, but the council admits that its aim is more to influence and educate the public rather than build a closely knit membership.

While struggling to create a distinct niche within a nonsecular society, secular humanists realize that they also have to cooperate with like-minded progressive and liberal religionists in order to find a hearing on many issues, which represents a departure from past eras when secularists condemned liberal and conservative belief systems equally. A history of the freethought movement in the United States has broadened its parameters to include liberal and nonconventional religionists who are viewed as being in agreement on issues such as women's rights, abortion, and strict church-state separation (Jacoby 2004). The Secular Student Alliance takes such a big-tent approach, including agnostics and others who support the values of secularism, free speech, and rational inquiry. McGrath (2004: 175) has cited the move to include agnostics in some secularist groups as a departure from a "past firm and principled commitment to the nonexistence of God, and the liberating impact of this belief." As we discuss in the next chapter, however, the condemnation of all religion has been revived with the new atheism.

The future prospects for organized atheism and secular humanism in drawing seekers may also be limited by competition from postmodern philosophy and criticism. *Free Inquiry* magazine has targeted postmodernism (while continuing to criticize traditional religion and occultism) since the 1990s for eclipsing the importance of reason, objective truth, and science. The Secular Student Alliance was founded in part because of concern for the fact that postmodern philosophy and relativism have wide appeal in academia, and thus the potential to influence the current generation of American students. Postmodernism is problematic for the religious and secular alike, since postmodern philosophy involves a critique not only of the religious narrative, but also of the secular scientific, rational, or antireligious narrative (Davie 2004). Postmodernism and rationalistic naturalism are, in a sense, in competition for domination of secular American mentalities (Levitt 2001).

THE EVANGELICALIZATION OF ATHEISM

The past and present of American secularism and evangelicalism suggests an alternating dance between protagonists and antagonists, with each claiming to be either embattled minorities or victors, depending on cultural obstacles or opportunities. Competition between evangelical Protestants and freethinkers was formative for both movements in the nineteenth and twentieth centuries. Aside from philosophers influenced by European rationalist and anticlerical movements, organized secularism was not widely active or popular in nineteenth-century America. Yet the stigma of "infidelity" served as a foil for Protestant preachers to keep their members in the fold, according to religious historian Martin Marty (1961). Marty notes that secularists "flattered the churches by imitation," as they ventured into publishing tracts, books, and periodicals for their cause. As noted earlier, the use of congregation-like activities and structures marked a segment of secularist groups (Campbell 1972). Evangelicals have continued to consider the contentious and disunited coalition of secular humanists and atheists as a formidable enemy, even when their numbers and influence have been minimal.

The attempt by secularists in the last three decades to revive and galvanize their own ranks through the adoption of their perceived opponents' strategies is evident on a linguistic level in the very term "secular humanist" (Sandler 2006). Rather than resisting the label "secular humanist" because it was used by evangelicals as a critique of secular culture, Paul Kurtz appropriated and embraced it (Kurtz, in fact, reappropriated the term "secular humanist," which was used by freethinkers in the 1960s) before the religious right began using it. In doing so, Kurtz tried to shift evangelicals' pejorative use of the label to a positive, defiant form of self-identification. New Christian right leader Tim LaHaye, who first defined "secular humanism" as an amorphous but conspiratorial movement, would eventually target Kurtz and the Council for Secular Humanism as the main architects of secular humanism (LaHaye 1984; LaHaye and Noebel 2000). That LaHaye would label secular humanism a conspiratorial movement is not surprising when one considers his background in the John Birch Society and the Council for National Policy (Goldberg 2007).

The evangelical claim that secular humanism is actually a religion most vividly suggests how the opposition has helped to shape the movement. Conservative Christian critics claim that secular humanism defends a clearly defined worldview where humanity, reason, and science are worshipped instead of God. They support this charge with U.S. Supreme Court decisions (e.g., *Torcaso v. Watkins, U.S. v. Seeger,* and *Widmar v. Vincent*) defining humanism as a religion, arguing that if secular humanism is a religion it should not have a privileged place in public schools or in the public square in general. This argument infuriated Kurtz and other secularists, such as Leo Pfeffer, who first introduced the concept of secular humanism into Supreme Court documents, as they insisted that secular humanism is only a philosophy built on reason and science, gives no place to any supernatural or "transnatural" reality, and should therefore not be considered a religion. This insistence on making a distinction between secular humanism and religion has revived old conflicts within the humanist family. The issue of whether humanism is a religion has become particularly prominent in *Free Inquiry*, occupying an increasing number of pages.

A sharp response to the controversy was aired in the fall 2002 issue of *Free Inquiry*, with its cover emblazoned with the headline, "Drawing Clear Boundaries: Secular and Religious Humanism." Throughout the issue, religious humanists are taken to task for their semantic and conceptual errors in using the term "religious," and are even accused of cowardice for hiding behind religious terminology "in order to be socially acceptable" by their disassociation from atheists. That some religious humanists, such as segments of the Unitarians and some younger members of the AHA, are using concepts such as spirituality is doubly troublesome for the secular humanists. But most importantly for secular humanists, the religious humanist, "simply by existing, gives aid and comfort to the prayer warriors," wrote *Free Inquiry* editor Tom Flynn. Indeed, LaHaye and other evangelicals cite religious humanist writings as proof that secular humanism is a religion (Flynn 2002: 41).

Evangelical Christians have also shaped secular humanism by providing an impetus for formally uncommitted secular people to become involved in secular humanist and atheist organizations. In our interviews we found that the transition from being an inactive or "nominal" secular individual to becoming involved in secular humanist groups and activism was often instigated by contact and growing concern with individuals and issues associated with the religious right. We found this tendency in interviews conducted in New York, as well as in much more evangelically oriented

Oklahoma. As Phyllis, a fifty-three-year-old New York educator and former leftist activist, said,

> I didn't know much about the religious right until I had to work with them. I started seeing what they were about and became very frightened at the rhetoric. I realized the Board of Education in New York is permeated with born-again Christians. The rhetoric was borderline fascist, with attacks on single mothers. I was harassed on the job when [they found out I was an atheist]. It was openly racist, and it was coming from black and Hispanic people. But the left wasn't serious about the born-again threat. The threat to the First Amendment was a nonissue for them. I always knew I was an atheist but never saw the need to talk about it until I saw how [these] people were threatening freedom.

The shock Phyllis felt—learning that her values diverged so strongly from those around her—inclined her toward political action and led her to come out as an atheist. Similar stories of secularists being spurred to action as a result of moral outrage and anger show how such emotions can be used as a basis for mobilization (Nepstad and Smith 1999).

The way in which secular humanists and atheists portray their position in society parallels patterns in Smith's (1998) study of American evangelicals. Smith found that the tensions and unease that evangelicals experience as they interact in the greater American society enhance the vitality of their religious identity. Oppositional relations and interactions between different groups generate and maintain a variety of subcultural identities in a pluralistic society. Portraying the group as a besieged minority may not strengthen group identity as effectively for secularists as for evangelicals for a variety of reasons, such as geographic dispersion and a personality trait of "openness"

(Shermer 1999), manifesting itself in a "less agreeable, more individualistic style" (Galen 2009: 45). Such openness at the personal level leads to more openness at the organizational level. This limits tendencies that would encourage the type of sectarianism and separatism that can be found among extreme religious subcultures as well as the strong organizational structures indicative of more mainstream, hierarchically oriented religions and churches in modern societies.

American evangelicals and believers tend to mobilize through friends and neighbors in a local community and church, which are strongly connected to broader mobilizations at the state and national level. Secularist organizations, on the other hand, tend to mobilize through a variety of different means: like-minded strangers online, local groups and meet-ups, blogs, talks, student alliances, and so on. In addition, the strong community ties of evangelicals coupled with an emphasis on "following the word of God" makes it easier to rally and align support for a particular political issue insofar as it is framed as a mandate from God. As an example, consider the turnout against gay marriage in California and the massive power that Rick Warren and the Mormon Church's efforts wielded therein, rallying believers for support of Proposition 8, banning gay marriage.

As was evident in our interviews, the perception that religious conservatives were winning the culture wars through their influence in the Bush administration also strengthened the secular humanist–atheist identity. Recent survey research suggests that the right-wing politicization of churches in the last two decades alienated a segment of liberal church members, who retreated from institutional religion into the ranks of the unchurched and thus added to the pool of potential secularists (Hout and Fischer 2002; Campbell 2013). Note that the *perception* of being embattled, regardless of the reality, can drive subcultural formation. The perception of being on the losing side of the culture wars can be found among both evangelicals and secular humanists alike. Interviewees would at times acknowledge the secular basis of most modern American institutions while asserting that they have little support from either the media or political and educational establishments in maintaining their secular worldview and lifestyle.

The centuries-old failure to maintain and increase a secularist organizational presence in the United States has been attributed to the secular nature of American government, where religious liberty and the separation of church and state prevented any need for anticlerical efforts to destroy the power of an oppressive state church, as was the case in Europe. As Colin Campbell (1972: 61) writes, "In the long run the secularists would have benefited from the sort of official persecution and opposition which they experienced in Britain and they would have certainly benefited from the existence of a state Church in that there would then have been a real possibility of uniting radical, political, and theological opinion." The growing public nature of religion, manifested most clearly in the culture wars, may well have generated the sense of opposition and anticlericalism that can support a viable secularist subculture, as has long been the case in Europe (Casanova 1994). For example, a correlation between the rise of the religious right and a backlash in the form of the growth of the religiously nonaffiliated, or "nones," and nonbelievers mobilizing has been suggested. "I am very sanguine about secularism in the U.S.," said an atheist we interviewed. "The number of secularists has been growing for a couple of decades, and that may be in part because many people were turned off by the overreaching of the religious right during the Falwell-Robertson-Bush era of the '90s and 2000s."

The globalization of religion could also serve as such a catalyst (Ormerod 2010). Consider the United Nations' effort to pass a "defamation of religion" law in the wake of a religious backlash at the publication of antireligious cartoons, or the prominent place that

September 11, 2001, and Islam occupy in the work of the new atheists. With globalization it has become increasingly evident that as the rest of the world modernizes, people are not necessarily becoming more secular.

Many of the atheists we interviewed and surveyed over the course of ten years of research regularly bemoaned the religiosity that pervades American culture. At the same time, however, there was an understanding that secularism had a strong presence as well.[1] It could be argued that the loss of power of the religious right with the election of Barack Obama in 2008 moved secularists symbolically a little closer to the center in America,[2] thus decreasing their cultural tension with the center at least at the elite levels of politics and the culture. However, at the same time, evangelical and right-wing populism have resurged (Lindsey 2007), most evident in the popular appeal and mass marketing of evangelicals like Joel Olsteen and Rick Warren, as well as the rise of the Tea Party politically. In addition, constituencies in some states want to downgrade the scientific status of evolution and promote the teaching of creationism or intelligent design in the classroom, with research suggesting it is occurring in spite of the Supreme Court declaring it unconstitutional (Berkman et al. 2008). Some states are passing or attempting to pass "academic freedom bills" to protect those teachers who wish to critique scientific theories being studied, including but not limited to evolution (National Center for Science Education 2013). We could cite many more examples, all of which secularists could and do use to incite anger, point blame, and ultimately mobilize, giving credence to the notion that they are embattled in a religious nation.

For secularists, the separation of the state and church is not separate enough. Many conservative evangelicals, on the other hand, would like to bring politics and religion into closer contact, arguing that separation between church and state was meant only to keep government out of religion, not religion out of government. For both groups, the question of whether America is secular or religious is not only about separation—or how strict or porous the church-state divide is—but about legitimizing and normalizing values and beliefs that are an important part of their individual and group identities.

PERFORMING ATHEISM AND IDENTITY POLITICS: BETWEEN SEPARATION AND EQUALITY

Right from the start, the 2012 Reason Rally in Washington, DC, set the tone that was to dominate the rest of the day. As the crowd was filtering in to the National Mall, a band fired up the crowd with a rousing song that lampooned the belief in "Jesus coming again," mixing it with sexual innuendo. As the assembled crowd clapped and sang along to other songs satirizing religion, a large costumed puppet figure of Jesus danced among spectators. "We're not here to bash anyone's faith, but if it happens, it happens," comedian and master of ceremonies Paul Provenza announced to laughter and applause at the outset of the event. The bashing and attacks on religion, mainly Christianity (in its evangelical and Catholic forms), happened as much if not more than positive portrayals of secularism and were in sync with new atheist leader and scientist Richard Dawkins's advice to "mock and ridicule" people's beliefs. When one of the authors asked an official from the Secular Students Alliance, a group prominent in organizing the event, about whether the ridiculing of religion was productive, he answered, "This is what we do."

The rally was billed by its organizers as the "largest secular gathering in human history," but it also revealed how organized atheism had gained a measure of unity, support, and traction in popular culture during the preceding decade. The rally, which was organized and sponsored by twenty atheist and secular humanist organizations, was widely reported to be a "coming-out party" for atheists to publicly declare their unbelief and demand a place for themselves at the table. These objectives were not much different than those of its 2002 predecessor event called the "Godless March on Washington," but the two gatherings had notable contrasts. The Reason Rally drew an attendance of over ten thousand (although secularists have tended to go with the highest estimates of twenty thousand), whereas the 2002 march barely attracted twenty-five hundred secularists. Dawkins, clearly the main attraction of the event (with the crowd chanting his name as he made his entrance to the stage), told the audience that the rally could represent the "tipping point" for atheism; the mass of people declaring their unbelief would help lead to a rising tide of "everyone else coming out" as atheists. The atheists' interest in showing their numerical strength was on display at the rally, with the frequent claim made that they represent 16 to 17 percent of the population (taken from survey results showing a growth of unaffiliated—though not necessarily secularist—America).

There was a much larger presence of young adults and women at the rally than in 2002; the founding of the Secular Student Alliance and its rapid growth in colleges and high schools (doubling since 2009 from 143 campuses to 350) may be a factor in that change. Much of the success of the rally can be credited to the greater coordination and unity between the various secularist groups, ranging from such veterans as the American Atheists and the Freedom from Religion Foundation to the influential Center for Inquiry

(CFI), Humanistic Judaism, and the well-funded Richard Dawkins Foundation.

In 2002 the fractious tendency of secularist groups was more evident, with several groups declining to participate. In 2012 even the more moderate American Humanist Association (AHA) took an active part in the rally; as AHA spokeswoman Maggie Ardiente told us in an interview, "Atheism is the first step on the path" to a more positive kind of humanism. The event featured the old standard-bearers of freethought; magician and veteran skeptic James Randi resembled a walking social type of the village atheist as he jabbed his cane toward the sky and railed against the "misogynistic, genocidal, sexist, racist, militaristic, and homophobic" deity of the Old Testament. But the rally also showed how the new atheism and its professionalized, if polemical, style has raised secularism's status in the worlds of entertainment and popular culture, a subject we will address in the next chapter. The rally's performers, such as singer and comedian Tim Minchin, the rock group Bad Religion, comedian Eddie Izzard, and Adam Savage of the *Mythbusters* TV show, blended hip and edgy humor and artistic sensibility in their atheist repertoires. These personalities and increasing numbers of other performers are prominent in the entertainment world while also finding a niche market among secularists, along with a host of bloggers with large followings.

The prominent role of celebrities and the calls for reason and coming out of the closet to claim a place in American society at the event were joined seamlessly with irreverent attacks on religion. The tension, if not conflict, between the secularists' strategies of debunking religion and calling for acceptance in a largely religious, if pluralistic, society was as apparent in 2012 as it was in 2002. This tension between celebrating and suppressing difference from a majority or norm is an issue with which many identity movements struggle (Bernstein 1997). Highlighting the difference from a religious majority can strengthen unity internally both positively (e.g., celebrating an intellectual superiority) and negatively (e.g., emphasizing the oppressiveness of religion). Highlighting similarities with a majority may broaden or extend a movement but may also decrease intensity within it. This question of how much attention to devote to internal issues, such as strengthening unity and increasing membership, versus reaching out and appealing or collaborating with other groups to achieve certain ends, is another issue that all movements have to grapple with and negotiate.

Moreover, agreeing that a problem exists and needs to be addressed, and motivating people to do so, is not to agree on what should be done or how to go about doing it. The issue of gender relations is a recent example in which secularists split into factions over political concerns. A secularist blogger issued a call for a "third wave" of atheism that would unite the politics of the left with a concern that women participants would be free of sexual harassment. She had in mind reports that women had been plagued with sexual harassment at atheist events, but the declaration ignited a bitter split whereby the leaders of the new movement, known as Atheism+, in effect excommunicated or "disowned" dissenters from its platform (McGrath 2012). This example highlights how moving from the abstract to the concrete can divide individuals within a particular group (some secularists have dismissed sexual harassment within the movement as a nonissue), which perhaps helps explain why secularists place so much emphasis on where they do agree. Also, until a constituency of like-minded people come together and decide to act, practical matters regarding strategies and goals are not really an issue. Focusing on broad areas of agreement is a first initial step in establishing a base, whereas getting too specific can turn subgroups against one another.

Research in human psychology suggests that individuals are more likely to act to avoid dire consequences than to seize new opportunities (Quattrone and Tversky 1988). And the threat of religion—whether in the form of the religious right and the threat of dissolving the separation of church or 9/11—is arguably one of the main triggers motivating secularists to act. The proclamation that they are not necessarily against religion but irrationalism may help, perhaps functioning to broaden appeal as well.

Many participants in these groups still believe that they are in the forefront of secularism and progress. Humor is an important device for declaring the superiority of freethought and secularism over religious thought. Moreover, humor can be used to gain mainstream acceptance. As Herbert, a humanist lawyer at the march, noted, "Nothing should be off limits. Why should religion get a pass? One of the ways to have a secular society is for people to be able to laugh at themselves. That's the important first step." He also added that the "absurdities of religion have to be exposed. Why shouldn't religion be held up for ridicule just because most people have [religious beliefs]? Why do we have to hush up just because more people believe than don't believe?" A forty-one-year-old atheist activist from California remarked, "We all make fun of everything, including freethought. In a free marketplace of ideas, everything is open to ridicule. If there is something that can't be made fun of, then there's something wrong."

As civil right struggles have shown, one of the ways social identities become politically salient is in opposition to discrimination, highlighting a discrepancy between the promise and the practice of the democratic process in respect to the (unequal) distribution of goods and rights. In the wake of the civil rights movement, many new groups—from feminists to gays to religious fundamentalists—have taken up the discourse of identity to struggle for equity and recognition in the political arena. Atheists are following suit in their claim that they are an embattled minority in need of rights and even protection in a religious and hostile society, tacitly acknowledging the failure of widespread secularism. Both *Free Inquiry* and as our interviews feature frequent use of language expressing a minority identity and status, often taken from minority and identity politics, calling for atheists and secular humanists to engage in greater activism to protect their rights.

This point was illustrated in an interview with Paul, a fifty-six-year-old businessman in the Washington, DC, area, during the Godless March on Washington in 2002. For Paul, the process of coming out as an atheist was gradual. He was raised in a conservative Lutheran home. "The first step is realizing that you don't believe what everyone else believes. Then this little voice in your head [starts] saying that you're going to hell.... The [next] step is saying, 'I'm an atheist,' and then saying, 'I'm an atheist and proud of it.' That's the more difficult step." In his own personal life, he said, "it's traumatic to be surrounded by a community that is hostile to you. It's not politically correct to disrespect blacks, gays, or the handicapped, but it's still all right to disrespect atheists.... Religious people are usually the extremists, and they represent a much larger group. But they consider us not to be fully human. One of the things that rule your life when you're an atheist is fear. You never know when you're going to be attacked." This fear is two-sided. On the one hand, it can lead to paralysis and apathy. On the other, it can lead to action. As the social movement literature suggests, the course such emotions take is contextual and would depend on whether resources and support are in place to channel such threats and anxieties into activism.

With greater exposure comes greater criticism. In recent years, several organizations, such as the Atheism Anti-Discrimination Support Network, have formed to counter discrimination and build a political identity. Addressing a New York secular humanist meeting, Margaret Downey, the network's director, said that she wanted to "empower the atheist community so we don't become easy victims of prejudice." Regarding one Christian television commentator who voiced a negative opinion on atheists, she commented, "We don't want to change her religious views, just her prejudice."

In the secularist movement's meetings, blogs, and online forums, much debate takes place about what name might make for a more positive self-image among Americans than atheist or secular humanist. The media devoted some attention to the effort among one group of atheists to substitute "Brights" for the older terms, but little agreement exists in practice on actually adopting that term (Shermer 2003). New atheist spokesman and scientist Richard Dawkins argued that adopting the name "brights" and forsaking the older designations would be an exercise in consciousness-raising (Dawkins 2003). Replacing derogatory terms of the past with more positive ones (or reappropriating them) is a tactic frequently employed by many once-stigmatized minority groups seeking to gain a place for themselves in American society, from African Americans to gay rights activists. One could even call such a move a standard strategy of contemporary identity politics. As Grant Farred (2000: 638) writes, "The struggle for identity has often turned on the capacity of marginalized groups to set their own political agenda, simultaneously acknowledge, reject, and reinscribe the disjuncture between 'identities imposed' and those desired."

Atheists want to mobilize to challenge and eliminate the stigma associated with nonbelief. However, in mobilizing and articulating claims they need to use the stigmatized identity they aim to change. In doing so, and in seeking recognition, they run the risk of strengthening the biased social category of nonbelief they aim to overturn insofar as it suffers from historical stereotypes and is

associated with negative characteristics and carries negative connotations. "This is a dilemma both at the level of means, of how to get
what you want, and at the level of ends, since moral dignity arises
both from abolishing the stigma and from organizing politically"
(Jasper 2010: 31). Sam Harris (2007) grapples with the dilemma
in his controversial "The Problem with Atheism" lecture, where he
suggests, "I think that 'atheist' is a term that we do not need, in the
same way that we don't need a word for someone who rejects astrol-
ogy.... All we need are words like 'reason' and 'evidence' and 'common sense' and 'bullshit' to put astrologers in their place, and so it
could be with religion." He adds,

> Another problem is that in accepting a label, particularly the
> label of "atheist," it seems to me that we are consenting to be
> viewed as a cranky sub-culture. We are consenting to be viewed
> as a marginal interest group that meets in hotel ballrooms. I'm
> not saying that meetings like this aren't important. I wouldn't be
> here if I didn't think it was important. But I am saying that as a
> matter of philosophy we are guilty of confusion, and as a matter
> of strategy, we have walked into a trap.

Harris suggests that any move toward an actual atheist movement is a step in the wrong direction—unnecessary at best, counterproductive at worst. His advice: "Go under the radar—for the rest
of your life and be [a] decent, responsible [person] who destroys
bad ideas wherever [you] find them." The notion that all atheists
need to do is *pass*, forming a covert community of fellow travelers,
and take to rooting out and combating bad ideas wherever they find
them within their personal lives is a point upon which not all atheists agree. "If we all came out, as Richard Dawkins advocates," one
respondent stated, "people might be surprised to learn who we are,

and that we are not the terrible people that they perhaps had previously stereotyped us as. Rather, we are your friends, and colleagues and family members, and run the gamut of personalities . . . just like everyone else!" Many also recognize that such advice neglects the role that institutions and the state play in the formation of the symbolic boundaries that marginalize nonbelievers in the United States. As an example, in comparing atheist activism to gay activism, one respondent asserted, "We are nowhere near as organized or as willing to be activists as the GLBT community. Shit, we barely have a lobby. This is a shame because the GLBT folks are a paradigm of how to change hearts and minds—and laws."

Over the course of the nineteenth and twentieth centuries, and into the twenty-first, America has recognized gender, race, and increasingly sexuality as illegitimate criteria for exclusion from participation and rights. All such progress—far from being a product of solely chipping away at bad ideas one by one—has involved groups of like-minded individuals banding together in distinct subcultures and counterpublics and ultimately forming public social movements to fight against the forces that subjugated them in order to change their subordinate status. Many atheists expressed this subordinate status in our personal interviews and questionnaires: "I think that freethinkers face many of the same challenges that homosexuals face—that is, being demonized by religious groups, ignored/disrespected by politicians, and ostracized by society in general."

Although such activism takes different organizational and expressive forms, the goal remains the same: inclusion and autonomy. This distinction between inclusion and autonomy runs throughout this book in various forms, from the disputes between those who favor accommodation versus those who prefer confrontation to the different expressive forms found in organizational activism versus the more grassroots orientations found among independents.

An example aiming at inclusion can be seen in the name change from the "National Atheist Party" to the "Secular Party of America." As the party's vice president of public relations and marketing Bernard Kellish noted, the change, aimed at gaining greater political traction and forming a broad coalition with other secular organizations, is "far more inclusive of a greater number of Americans that share our vision of true separation of church and state…[opening] the door to those that may not have joined us if for no other reason than because 'Atheist' was in the name" (Anne 2013). As the statement on the opening page of their homepage read at the time of the name change,[3]

> The Secular Party of America seeks to politically represent all Americans who share the goal of a secular government by gathering the political strength of secularists nationwide, while being guided by the values of secular humanism and evidenced-based reasoning. The Secular Party of America is a Constitutional movement dedicated to the preservation of the Founding Fathers' vision of a secular nation. We are a progressive secular political organization whose current incarnation is a nonprofit 527 political organization. As we grow and evolve, we intend and expect to develop into a full-fledged political party. We are assembled for two important reasons: to give a political voice to U.S. secularists, who have never enjoyed political representation before, and to stand against those elements and groups that would seek to undermine the secular foundations of this great country.

In seeking to tie itself strongly with America's past and "seeking to represent all Americans," the Secular Party, as well as other inclusive-oriented organizations like the Secular Coalition, seek to promote a more mainstream and palatable identity for nonbelievers, hoping to counteract the notion that to be a secularist (read "atheist") is un-American. In making the primary issue the separation of church and state and making the enemy "those elements and groups that would seek to undermine the secular foundations of this great country," such as the religious right, they seek to project and promote themselves as part of a broader public and aim to align themselves with the larger movement of those Americans—including religious liberals—who disapprove of the strong influence of religion in government.

At the same time, secularist groups have pushed in the other direction, toward more autonomy and cultural self-determination fueled by a more robust and radical critique of religion and the promotion of atheism as a primary, proud, and publicly professed identity. As one commenter responding to the name change asserted, "I'm proud to be an Atheist and want to be represented by other proud Atheists.... If an Atheist is afraid of calling themselves an Atheist then they will never be able to represent me or those like me."

When it comes to secularist identity politics, a segment of secular humanists and atheists oppose the recent trend of using the language of minority politics to describe their relation to American society (Nisbet 2007). This point is stressed in a *Free Inquiry* article by D. J. Grothe and Austin Dacey (2004) titled "Atheism Is Not a Civil Rights Issue":

> Civil rights struggles are related to a more general approach to social action known as "identity politics." In identity politics, people organize around their shared identity rather than their party affiliation or political ideology. This is quite appropriate for groups whose collective, historical experience of oppression has forged some substantial unity in belief and social agenda. Yet

atheists have no beliefs in common but their disbelief. Imagine a voting bloc that would back a candidate merely for lacking faith in a personal deity.

While these authors, as outspoken atheists, agree with the ends of promoting and institutionalizing a social and political culture more hospitable to nonbelief, they disagree with the means of those who would wish to use or focus on their identity as secularists to do so, making the case that secularists (or de facto atheists) have no group-specific traits in common but their disbelief. Many atheists agree with this point, most prominently Christopher Hitchens and Sam Harris. However, other atheists ultimately feel that identity politics is appropriate for atheists, pointing out that there is no reason to automatically assume that racial or sexual identity group membership should be any more primary than an interest or ideological affiliation based in nonbelief. Identity commitments vary, be they ascribed or chosen, and groups are more or less coherent under different circumstances and contexts. Membership in a racial group, for example, may or may not be as important to a particular individual as that person's nonbelief. Moreover, identity is not a hard-clad, mutually exclusive category. As a recent billboard campaign—featuring the images of famous historic black "freethinkers," such as the social reformer Frederick Douglass and the writer Zora Neale Hurston, and news stories highlighting African American atheists' influential role in the civil rights movement—attests, one can be black and an atheist. Identity, empirically understood, is a complex matter that has performative aspects and involves switching or emphasizing certain aspects of one's identity and downplaying others depending on the context. Rather than arguing that organizing around certain identities is only appropriate for certain actions, secularists' strategies and actions show that all identities have public and political potential, in spite of their varied collective histories—which inevitably change over time and across space.

The exclusion of certain personal commitments and identity claims from politics—a central tenet of the American liberal democratic system—has helped justify the political marginalization of various groups. In fact, all of the aforementioned groups—from women to blacks—gained recognition in the court of public opinion and the realm of law, using the language of rights as leverage, by politicizing issues previously considered private or a matter of personal conscience. This exclusion of certain personal commitments from politics, promoted under the banner of neutrality, informs the separation of church and state. Such separation is driven by the idea that a nation that includes various groups of individuals with passionately held ideals and religious beliefs can only be expected to reconcile such commitments by allowing them to be exercised privately. Such neutrality is a bit double-edged with regard to atheist activism. On the one hand, this neutrality—and the establishment clause that backs it—functions to blunt the more extreme goals of certain religious activists insofar as it keeps any particular religion from exercising its will within the halls of power, giving atheists the legal leverage to contest and strike down certain laws that do not meet the *Lemon* test. At the same time, however, this norm of neutrality—encapsulated in the cliché so many of us heard from our parents: "You never discuss politics or religion in public"—works to shield religion from the full critique many atheists feel it rightly deserves—not just within the realm of law but within everyday political discourse.

American civil society, based on egalitarian principles of pluralism, is made up of individuals with shifting political identities and commitments. While some secularists defend Grothe and Dacey's point, other secularists find no reason to argue that the collective identity of certain individuals is legitimate for political participation while others are not. As a case in point, secularists have collectively come together to form a secularist political party, with the hope and goal of electing unapologetically atheist candidates someday. Regardless of what side any secularist comes down on, this matter is ultimately a matter for secularists on the ground in real time as historical social actors to decide for themselves. Moreover, while Grothe and Dacey want to use a group's status as historical "victims" as the yardstick by which one determines whether identity politics is appropriate, secularists such as Edward Tabash (2004) and David Koepsell (2007) have argued that there is plenty of discrimination and prejudice of nonbelief and irreligion to make the opposite case and come to the opposite conclusion. While secularist organizations at the national level—such as the Secular Party, the Secular Coalition for America, and the Freedom from Religion Foundation—continue to lobby for and defend the wall of separation, atheists are beginning to follow the LGBT activists in using equal-protection arguments, the same argument gays have used to legalize marriage in some states.[4]

THE NONBELIEVER NICHE

The expansion of atheist and secular humanist organizations, publications, and websites in recent years suggests that they may be filling a niche vacated by religious humanists, Unitarians, and other liberal religious groups that have taken a greater interest in spirituality. It can be argued that there is a "demand" for secular humanism among a small minority of Americans, even if the "supply" for such individualistic consumers would obviously be less stable and rigorous (or strict) than that found among religious niches (Stark and Finke 2000).

Supply-side theory sees competition as a mechanism for reinforcing group solidarity, predicting that individuals express higher levels of commitment under conditions of fierce competition and lower levels under conditions where a particular group more or less holds a monopoly. Subcultural theory holds a similar view regarding conflict strengthening group solidarity. There is some validity to both the notion of secularists filling a niche and that of conflict working to enhance commitment. A recent study seems to confirm these theories, finding that the prevalence of conservative Christians in a given area of the United States predicts the establishment of a secularist organization (Garcia and Blankholm 2013). But this may be only one side of the equation. The other has to do with resources. An unpublished study coauthored by one of the authors (Perl and Cimino 2011), for example, found that membership rates in two national organizations advocating for strong separation were lower in areas that voted Republican and areas where nonbelievers filed higher numbers of lawsuits to protect their religious freedom (or their freedom from religion in these cases), lending support to the resource mobilization paradigm. This theory argues that activism will be strongest where there are substantial resources to draw upon, beginning with a population sympathetic to the cause. In other words, "far from being strongest in areas where the religious right is prominent, pro-secular groups may thrive in politically liberal areas where the government already tends to protect the rights of non-religious people from religious encroachment" (Perl and Cimino 2011: 1). As the case of evangelicals shows, competition and resources are both important for success (hence the notion that they are embattled yet thriving).

Competition, whether among the various nontheist groups, or between a secular group and a religious organization (such as Unitarian-Universalism), has encouraged innovations and organization-building, as can be seen in the formation of secular humanist self-help and relief organizations. The modest degree of tension between organized secular humanism and atheism and the wider society likewise increases commitment to the nontheist cause, even if the individualism and weak social ties of participants mitigate against forming strong intergenerational community ties and loyalty (Bainbridge 2005; Cragun et al. 2012). In its recent history, secular humanism has reasserted its identity and strengthened its boundaries by differentiating itself from religious humanism, Unitarian-Universalism, and secular postmodernism, on the one hand, and a newer confrontationist atheism, on the other. At the same time, because secular humanism and atheism both draw on a very small market share, these movements have attempted to expand the secular niche to include agnostics, experimented with the use of rituals and rites of passage, and built coalitions with liberal religious groups on various social issues. Their adoption of both the subcultural style of evangelicals and identity politics allows secular humanists and atheists to press for greater acceptance in American society while maintaining a vital subculture.

In conclusion, the secular humanist and atheist patterns of interaction and conflict discussed in this chapter suggest that these freethinkers' hopes and visions of a secular America have been severely modified for the purpose of sustaining an identity within a religious (though pluralistic) society. In fact, the real and imagined culture wars and the forging of a subcultural identity may turn out to benefit the secular humanist and atheist movement far more than the much-hoped-for eclipse of faith and dawn of a humanist twenty-first century.

Chapter 2

The New Atheism and the Revival of Secularism

We started our research in the early 2000s under the assumption that organized atheism was facing an uphill battle against religious vitality in the United States. We weren't alone in that judgment. It was as recently as 2004 that evangelical historian and theologian Alister McGrath performed the last rites for atheism. Although considering the movement important enough to devote a book to it, McGrath wrote that the conciliatory mood of atheists, allowing agnostics to join their ranks, was a departure from a "past firm and principled commitment to the nonexistence of God, and the liberating impact of this belief." McGrath concluded that atheism had lost its cutting edge and was now trying to expand its numbers in a period of decline and diminished morale (McGrath 2004: 175; Bullivant 2010).

Only a few years later, McGrath had to reconsider his prognosis as a phenomenon called the "new atheism" racked up unprecedented book sales and media attention; in fact, he joined the growing ranks of evangelical writers issuing books responding to the new atheism.[1] As we discussed in the last chapter, many secularists themselves felt that their days were numbered and were busy employing new strategies for survival, one of which was casting themselves as

53

a new minority group that needed protection in a religious society. Although these strategies still hold, atheism has become more popular and is undergoing something of a revival in Western societies. Of course, it wasn't only the new atheism associated with such names as Richard Dawkins and Christopher Hitchens that created a groundswell of publicity and interest in secularism. In the last chapter we discussed the growing rate of nonaffiliation and the disenchantment with political religion in the United States that created a new audience and space for nonreligion and atheism. But such an explanation doesn't account for the popularity of atheism even in European countries with high rates of secularity and little religious opposition.

THE MEDIUM IS THE ATHEIST MESSAGE

In this chapter we argue that viewing the new atheism as a media-driven phenomenon best explains the reach and greater public presence. The best-selling books by Richard Dawkins, Daniel Dennett, Christopher Hitchens, and Sam Harris[2] form the "canon" of the new atheism, but media in the form of magazines, websites, blogs, online forums, and other books have also played an important role in driving this social phenomenon. This is especially the case with new media; they have created new forms of interaction and communication between secularists who may feel isolated in their communities. Secularists' recognition of their commonality and their desire "to construct a more satisfying culture" goes hand in hand with the expansion and development of collective practice (Wallace 1970: 188). In highlighting the role of media, we look at both the content and the medium. An analysis of articles on the new atheism in two secularist magazines, coupled with an Internet survey of self-identified atheists on the new atheism and their use of the media, allows us to see how secularists themselves are interpreting and evaluating the new atheism.

In examining the relation between current technology and modern experience, we use medium theory, which enables us to look at what is unique regarding the new atheism in strict relation to more general tendencies associated with our current conditions of communication. Medium theory situates these interpretations and evaluations in a broader media context, since they result from the process of mediation that secularists themselves go though in defining and understanding themselves as secularists. Instead of viewing technology as a tool solely for sending information among subjects who stand outside the technological apparatus, medium theorists are unique in arguing that technology and media should be seen as constituting an environment, or the material terrain, on and through which social knowledge and the social world itself are actively experienced and shaped.

Supporters of the new atheism have hailed the phenomenon as a harbinger of advancing secularism. The stigma of being an atheist was likely weakening even before the emergence of the new atheism; there had been a growth of organizations and activism among secularists attempting to make a place for themselves in American society by the turn of the millennium. Although it is unlikely that secularists were ever united in their strategies, a historical study by Bradly Nabors (2009) examines how atheists by the 1980s had significantly decreased their focus on fighting for church-state separation and had gradually stressed the role of argument and debate in making the atheist case. Nabors argues that the decline of the denominational society, where secular groups built coalitions with religions in order to legally defend their interests against a perceived dominant religious body (whether Protestant or Catholic), has given atheists less political legitimacy. For this reason, atheism has attempted to "regain this legitimacy by associating itself with science" and actively trying to discredit religious belief.

The sociology of media has just begun to address the issue of atheism. However, the past and contemporary literature on the public sphere (Habermas 1989; Calhoun 1992; Fraser 1992; Poster 1996) and the role media play in its constitution reveal an affinity with the study of minority and marginalized groups. Such groups perceive themselves to be excluded from dominant publics, communicate about that exclusion, and construct oppositional discourses through media and the formation of "counterpublics" (Negt and Kluge 1993; Fraser 1992). Keith Taylor (2006) examines how the Internet has created a forum for interaction and discussion of specific problems that atheists face in America. Similar use of media for defense (Unsigned 2008), entertainment (Adler 2007), public relations (Lyall 2009), and outreach (Simon 2008) has been covered in various newspapers and magazines.

Initial scholarly work on the phenomenon of the new atheism focused predominantly on the popular and media "response" (Koch 2008) or played a role in critiquing the new atheist authors (Amarasingam 2010). Such interpretive and critical studies offered significant insight regarding the actual content of the books and the responses they have generated. More recent studies have looked at the phenomenon in particular contexts (e.g., see *Approaching Religion* 2, no. 1 [2012] for some examples). They fail, however, to examine the larger media environment within which the books and all the commentary they have generated are formulated. In looking at this environment, we draw on medium theory to define media as the empirical-technical conditions of communication that allow certain forms of social interaction and ways of being while discouraging others (Innis 1984; McLuhan 1964; Meyrowitz 1985, 1994,

2000). In addition, we also look at the ways in which media interact with one another, understanding that cultural content has different influences when placed in different media and that changes in a media environment encourage new forms of content and interaction. To put it simply, if the new atheist books had been published prior to the advent of radio and television (to say nothing of the Internet), their influence as cultural content would have had a completely different influence (in terms of distribution, interpretation, etc.).

Examining the content and the media environment in which this content is received and circulated allows us to address questions concerning how media are reshaping relationships among atheists themselves, as well as altering the symbolic boundaries between atheists and theists. Textual analysis and medium theory both offer insightful approaches for studying atheism, seeing how the analysis of the one fits into and helps fill out the analysis of the other.

In looking at how the new atheist phenomenon has been interpreted and appropriated by those involved in atheist and secular humanist organizations, we analyze articles on the new atheism that have appeared in two of the most prominent secularist publications, *Free Inquiry* and the *American Atheist*, between January 2006 and March 2008—the period when the new atheism was at its peak in book sales and media attention. *Free Inquiry* is published by the Council for Secular Humanism, the main group of secular humanists. The *American Atheist* is published by American Atheists, an organization of approximately four thousand members founded by Madelyn Murray O'Hair in 1963. Second, we analyze and discuss responses to an online questionnaire (containing both open-ended and closed-ended questions) on the new atheism that we circulated among secular humanist and atheist organizations.

SECULARIST VIEWS ON THE NEW ATHEISM

We found that in the majority of articles in both *Free Inquiry* and the *American Atheist*, the new atheism was viewed as a positive development demonstrating the relevance and persuasiveness of the atheist message to American society. A significant minority of articles in both publications, however, criticized the style and substance of the new atheism, either for being too radical or not radical enough. The publication of the new atheist books was followed by and commented upon most frequently in *Free Inquiry*, which is not unusual considering the amount of space the magazine devotes to debating the public image and strategies of freethinkers in general. Virtually all of the new atheist authors contributed to *Free Inquiry* before their best-selling books were published. Dawkins has been particularly active in the secular humanist movement, speaking and writing against religion and promoting atheist identity (i.e., consciousness-raising for freethinkers by using the designation "brights").

The new atheism was treated as an emerging phenomenon by atheists and secular humanists only after Dawkins's book *The God Delusion* had become a bestseller and linked by the media with Harris's, Dennett's, and (later) Hitchens's books as the movement's touchstones. Since material in these books were extended versions of articles run by *Free Inquiry* since its inception, the new atheist literature was treated by the magazine mainly as a way of popularizing the atheist message, as well as a means of legitimizing secularism in American society. The tension between, on the one hand, spreading secularism and attempting to expose the fallacies of belief, and, on the other, seeking acceptance in a largely religious society runs through the recent history of secular humanism and is evident in secular humanists' treatment of the new atheism.

Free Inquiry was an early and enthusiastic booster of the new atheists. Starting in 2007 the new atheists' books were grouped together as a single phenomenon and were seen to represent a new stage of secularist assertiveness. Norm Allen, the director of African Americans for Humanism, wrote that the new atheists are following in the path of the abolitionists and other "radicals" throughout American history who have sought to "accelerate the agenda of moderates." Allen added that moderates who believe in dialogue with theists should not stand in the way of "radicals" such as Dawkins and Harris "who are taking atheism and naturalism to the masses in a way that's seldom been seen in this century" (Allen 2007: 52). In the same issue of *Free Inquiry*, Christopher Hitchens (2007a) defended the new atheism against criticisms that it represented a new fundamentalism in its attacks on religion. Hitchens wrote that such a "time-wasting tactic" devised by religious fundamentalists may appeal to "moderates" who want to appear even-handed, but it is a diversion from the argument against fundamentalism and theism.

One of the strongest and earliest affirmations of the new atheism in *Free Inquiry* came from its editor, Paul Kurtz (2007: 5), who noted that the magazine was "gratified" that several of its writers and their views were finding a wider audience, though he criticized the media's use of the term "evangelical atheism" to describe the phenomenon. Kurtz strongly refused to concede to the media criticism that the new atheist authors were unfairly attacking religion and religious people, adding that such authors were paying the price for "breaking the long-standing American taboo of not critically examining religion and calling into question the existence of God." Kurtz added that the "war against secularism by the religious right is unremitting; why should the non-religious, nonaffiliated, secular minority of the country remain silent?"

Along with the support for the new atheism, there was some wariness about the consequences of the unrelenting attack on religion. In a later editorial, Kurtz himself sounded a cautionary note, restating his longtime concern that secular humanists not be known as "nabobs of negativity," defined by the beliefs they oppose rather than for their positive system of ethics and philosophy (Kurtz 2007: 4). In fact, Kurtz's disquiet over the new atheism would intensify over the next few years and become a major factor in his dismissal from the leadership of CFI in 2009. Perhaps the sharpest critique of the new atheism was written by a British contributor in a symposium on the future of secularism in "post-Christian" Europe. Philosopher Julian Baggini (2007: 42–43) wrote that the "shock-and-awe tactics" of Dawkins and Dennett are "bound to fail," producing a polarization that could radicalize believers even more:

> Secularists have also misjudged the mood of the people they have purportedly liberated. People who once lived under the yoke of oppressive religion now have the freedom to believe, read, and do what they want. So why have the ungrateful bastards not become full-fledged atheists? The answer from some quarters seems to be that not all have got the message, so what they need is some reeducation in the folly of religion and the joys of science.

Baggini added that the new atheist strategy of blaming religion for most of the world's ills "just isn't credible. Images of murderous inquisitors just don't square with the English impression of tea with kindly vicars and genteel carol services at Christmas. In summary, we are wrong to respond to the rise of religion by squaring off for the big fight. To protect secularism we need to win the hearts and the minds of the moderate majority."

One would think that self-designated atheists would be far more supportive of the new atheism than secular humanists, who view atheism as only one component of their identity. An analysis of the *American Atheist*, however, suggests a similar level of support but more ambivalence than is found in *Free Inquiry*. There was less frequent citation of new atheist books in the *American Atheist*, most likely due to the fact that its authors are outside of the network of activists and writers who make up its parent organization, American Atheists. It could also be that the oppositional position of the new atheists was assumed in the *American Atheist*, and that there was an attempt to feature more diverse voices on the phenomenon.

The more activist thrust of American Atheists and its magazine tended to color the coverage of the new atheism in a political direction. In a 2008 editorial American Atheists president Ellen Johnson cited the popularity of the new atheist books (and her own media appearances) as helping to educate and mobilize nonreligious voters to the polls to press for their own rights. One article cited the usefulness of new atheist books in activism and recruitment for the cause, although the writer doubted that religious people will be exposed to such arguments even if they are authored by "big name atheists." Rather, what is needed is for ordinary atheists to "come out of the closet" and directly confront religious truth claims in their local media (Bice 2007: 21–23).

In a strongly positive review of Hitchens's *God Is Not Great*, one author argued that each of the new atheists' books can serve specific purposes: "I like to visualize a pair of 'good-cop, bad-cop' teams of interlocutors going forth to do battle with believers of all stripes. I would send Christopher Hitchens along with 'good cop' Daniel Dennett to do battle with the theologians and apologists" (Guadia 2008: 30). Even the favorable articles criticized the new atheists on a number of points, such as their tendency to target the Judeo-Christian God while ignoring the deities of other religions. An article by Indian rationalist author Meera Nanda (2008) focused on Harris's espousal of some aspects of Eastern spirituality (even as he attacks the monotheistic religions, especially Islam). Nanda charged that in his book, *The End of Faith*, Harris "loads spiritual practices with metaphysical baggage, all the while claiming to stand up for reason and evidence. By the end of the book, I could not help thinking of him as a Trojan horse for the New Age.... It is hard to believe that the author of this stuff is the most celebrated rationalist of our troubled times" (The uneasiness and questions about Harris's "secular spirituality" have since become a frequent concern among secular humanists and atheists [see Hoffmann 2006].) A 2008 cover story in the *American Atheist* titled "Is Dawkins Deluded?" was more critical of the doyen of atheism than most articles found in *Free Inquiry*. While agreeing with Dawkins more than its provocative headline might indicate, Massimo Pigliucci asserted that Dawkins's equating early religious education with child abuse was "downright pernicious," a charge that could be turned against Unitarians and even some nontheist groups while ignoring the critical thinking encouraged in some religious traditions (Pigliucci 2008: 17).

The respondents to our questionnaire clearly joined the above authors in affirming the new atheism and the way it legitimized and affirmed their identities as secularists. But only a small minority of the respondents were familiar, let alone identified, with the "new atheism" as a specific movement. Rather, their identification was with the new atheist authors and their best-selling books, and with the fact that they reached a mainstream readership and thus helped create for them new public acceptance and engagement with the cause of atheism. Almost all respondents had read at least one of the new atheist books, and the sense of acceptance they reported was also related to the belief that the new atheism was helping to dispel forms of belief that were especially intolerant toward atheists. One respondent noted that he was "glad" about the new acceptance, adding, "I think many people are tired of the bullying by the Religious Right." Others believed that this sense of greater security might be short-lived. As one respondent wrote, "I expect a stronger pushback if [these books] become more popular (I am in Oklahoma!)." The only respondent who felt no such sense of acceptance wrote that "individuals who base their life on...mythology are unable to confront reality. Actually, for such individuals with immature minds, the more vocal and public we are, the more threatened they feel, and act." Although more than half of respondents believed that atheists are still discriminated against, few could cite incidents where they personally felt such prejudice. One reason is that no external markers or signifiers announce someone as an atheist, making it easier for atheists to avoid any social stigma by keeping their nonbelief to themselves. Another factor is that the prejudice atheists *as a social group* face in the United States tends to be more of an institutional or structural sort than of an individual or explicitly discriminatory or violent sort—due in some part to the aforementioned point—although there have been cases of more individual and violent incidents, with atheists receiving death threats, getting kicked out of apartments, and losing their jobs.

Interestingly, even though the media have portrayed these books as hostile and negative toward religious believers, over half of the respondents were of the view that theists who read them would have a more positive view of atheists and atheism. Some did wonder how many religious people would actually read such books, and if they might offend their friends and relatives. But the contentious nature of the new atheism was more often considered one of its major draws, regardless of whether theists, society, or the media approved of it. As one respondent wrote, "We have been too nice to the religious for decades and it has gotten us nowhere....A plain no-nonsensical statement of our views is long overdue. Dawkins [and] Hitchens are my heroes where this is concerned." While the media were praised for introducing new atheist views, respondents also noted that atheism still faces media discrimination and disregard. "Atheism has always been cast in the lowest regard by the media and most everyone in America. I tend to be more outspoken now [after the new atheist books] than ever before. I now refuse to just nod my head to religious conversations and say nothing to irritate those conversing," one respondent wrote.

If the mainstream media were viewed in a critical light, there was more support and affirmation concerning the Internet (twenty-four of the thirty-four respondents who answered the question about the mainstream media showed such negative views). The substantial transformations in our contemporary communication technologies are creating a new way for atheists to come out, speak out, and meet up in a still largely religious society. The responses to the questionnaires went some way toward confirming this point. Since our sample came from the contact lists of secular humanist and other secularist groups, it was expected that most were active in organized secularist groups. But among the active respondents (which could mean anything from attending an occasional meeting or meet-up with other atheists), Internet activity often supplemented their offline involvement. There was also a degree of movement between exclusive Internet activity and contact and offline involvement in secularist groups and activism (about 20 percent of the sample). However, a significant minority (approximately 40 percent) reported solely online involvement, usually in the form of visiting favorite websites and interacting with other atheists in forums and by e-mail. A Colorado man who went from Internet involvement to offline activity said, "The great thing about the Internet is that if you want to come out you can, and if you want to get a message out but don't want to be known to the world you can do so anonymously as well. I think that is a great start for people who are reluctant to come out officially." The weak ties that the Internet generates and that seem to make up the secularist community in the United States permit discussion and interaction on topics such as the new atheism, creating an inviting environment for nontheists to be more outspoken and involved in group activity with like-minded freethinkers, a subject we explore in chapter 3. Such interactions led to more optimistic attitudes about the progress of secularism in American society and the decline of the influence of religion. More than half of the respondents believed that secularism was growing and religion fading, although an element of conflict was present in these accounts. A respondent said that atheism/secularism "is very slowly gaining acceptance as people become disenchanted with the [religious right] attempting to legislate their beliefs into laws. Blue laws are rarely enforced,... Antiabortionist groups are increasingly being marginalized as wacky and their zeal is losing sympathy from outsiders who were on the sidelines." This greater optimism contrasted with the ethnographic interviews presented in chapter 1, where there was marked pessimism about the state of secularism in society. This change, which is also evident in the pages of *Free Inquiry* and *American Atheist*, may also be related to the changeover to a Democratic administration and the real and perceived losses to the Christian right.

A MEDIATED REVIVAL OF ATHEISM

As a social phenomenon, the new atheism effectively enhanced atheism's profile. Prior to the new atheism, its only presence in American popular culture was negative news coverage of American Atheists' founder and atheist activist Madalyn Murray O'Hair. On the whole, historically speaking, interest in atheism has largely been expressed outside the cultural mainstream and within specialized academic, theological, and legal circles. The new atheist books, on the other hand—coupled with an institutional network of secularist publications, organizational newsletters, and various magazines through which the phenomenon was initially given shape—have propelled atheism into the public square. Not only have numerous books by openly avowed atheists made bestseller lists for the first time in U.S. history, but films and TV shows with firm and explicit antireligious sympathies and sentiments have also emerged, such as *Religulous* and *Family Guy*. In fact, comedians have been very influential in popularizing the new atheist critique to a mass audience. Comedians such as Billy Connolly, Bill Maher, Eddie Izzard, Ricky Gervais, Louis C.K., David Cross, and Julia Sweeney, to name just a few, use sharp invective as much as satire and sarcasm against religion. Such entertainers have broken the taboo of questioning and negotiating the "taken-for-grantedness" of religion, according to Douglas Cowan. As comedians, like other entertainers, have gained the status of authorities in our celebrity culture, they have "joined the cultural pool of 'conversational' experts . . . reinforcing our beliefs when we agree with them, forcing us to shore up our beliefs when we don't" (Cowan 2013: 34–36). An impressive array of secondary literature has also appeared in the form of magazine and newspaper articles, TV news coverage, Internet blog posts, and podcasts, as well as academic publications, conferences, and debates. In addition, many public critics, including evangelical leaders and laity, have read and responded to these books (McGrath 2007; Mohler 2008; Aikman 2008; Marshall 2007; Hedges 2008).

Scholars have noted how the market has been fragmented, with cultural producers engaging in more and more niche marketing. That targeting more specific identity groupings has proven profitable opened up the publishing houses to take a chance on the new atheist texts. And with the success of the new atheist texts, a broader spectrum of publishers targeting more diverse secularists are looking to capitalize on the trend, with veteran, upstart, and academic presses all releasing numerous books on the topic within recent years and more slated for the near future. In addition, some titles originate with bloggers and are at first self-published (Winston 2013).

The publication and success of these new atheist texts, which are written for a popular audience, provide its advocates with an open-ended project with which to identify, creating a shared vision, even if the messages of each individual author vary. Creating a general vernacular and a broadly accepted set of ideas helps temper sectarian tendencies among highly individualist secularists and provides them with a base of general interest. This, in turn, allows secularists to start imagining themselves as part of a broader community "out there" (apart from a specific sense of place and local meet-up group, for example), even though they will likely never meet many, if any, of their fellow secularists (Anderson 1991). This sense of reading with like-minded strangers provides secularists with a greater sense of acceptance. At the same time, their sense of being a minority is intensified in today's media environment, as secularists are continuously reminded that religious adherence persists alongside their own new forms of publicity. Drawing on Marshall McLuhan's global village metaphor, Joshua Meyrowitz writes,

As the membranes around spatially segregated arenas [have] become more *informationally* permeable, through television and other electronic media, the current trend is toward integration of all groups into a relatively common experiential sphere—with a new recognition of the special needs and idiosyncrasies of *individuals*. (Meyrowitz and Maguire 1993: 43, emphasis added)

In such a scenario, experience is "deterritorialized," or cut off from a particular place, tradition, or group; the boundaries of those whom we perceive and experience as significant are radically redefined.

Georg Simmel introduced his concept of the stranger to explain the contradictory experience of what it means to be both near and far simultaneously. As Simmel explains,

> The unity of nearness and remoteness involved in every human relation is organized in the phenomena of the stranger, in a way which may be most briefly formulated by saying that in the relationship to him, distance means that he, who is close by, is far, and strangeness means that he, who is also far, is actually near. (Simmel 1950: 402–403)

Secularists can be considered strangers in two ways. First, in a strictly spatial sense they can be considered strangers in crossing a boundary and entering a space where they were previously not visible to the degree they are now. Second, in a symbolic sense, as Edgell et al. (2006) show, they are positioned as distant from the norm of American religiosity, while actively and symbolically stationing themselves apart and antagonistically against such a norm. Of course, Simmel's understanding of "strangeness" involved being co-present in a particular geographic locale. Yet, with the advent of modern media, being close socially does not necessarily require geographic proximity. For example, as Anderson argued in *Imagined Communities* (1991), the advent of the newspaper (coupled with standardized vernacular) opened up the possibility to conceive of community in larger terms beyond the scope of a particular locale grounded in face-to-face communication and the co-presence of subjects as the necessary basis of social and communal relations.

This transition from place- to space-based forms of interaction and communication with our contemporary media landscape does not negate Simmel's insights regarding the tension between near and far. And if we consider our electronic media environment to constitute, at least theoretically, an all-inclusive arrangement where all individuals and groups may be considered strangers to one another, we can see how there are no mainstream culture or host groups in such a "place" when the "center is everywhere." Tension or distance have not necessarily been eased or erased, though. In fact, granting individuals and groups once firmly separated (by geography as well as social status and roles) access to the same experiential space heightens awareness of social and symbolic similarities and discrepancies (Meyrowitz and Maguire 1993).

Before the electronic age, secularists could read popular and scholarly works proclaiming the inevitable demise of religion and believe that the secularization of society—to the extent that it was causally linked to modernization—was merely a matter of time. Sociologists overwhelmingly held and spread such a view. The situation is quite different today. Secularists of all ages see American religiosity sprawled across billboards and proudly displayed in many televised religious, political, and sporting events, to say nothing of the religiosity of the rest of the world that is transmitted into their homes on nightly news programs. Moreover, widely publicized opinion polls continue to confirm for secularists the fact that the United States—although in practice and theory a secular state—is made up of a population in which a significant majority considers belief in God the norm, with a seemingly endless fascination with the supernatural, as evident in numerous television shows and films about ghosts, ghost hunting, and other paranormal events. Perhaps more seriously, polls continue to verify that a majority of Americans are skeptical about the scientific merits and soundness of evolution, and favor the teaching of creationism alongside evolution in school, which is often discussed in local newspapers and newscasts across the country. This notion that social and informational integration may intensify the perception of segregation is in line with what we found in our research (discussed in chapter 1), in which most participants in secular and atheist groups made the transition from being an inactive or "nominal" secular individual to becoming involved in secular humanist groups and activism through contact and growing concern with individuals and issues associated with the religious right.

A growing concern about religion, usually of the conservative variety, in the public square and political sphere, coupled with an increased desire to act, is also consistent with what we found in the responses to our questionnaire. One respondent, for example, stated that he "started donating more money to humanist organizations after seeing clips of the film 'Jesus Camp' & the CNN TV series, 'God's Warriors.'" In this context, the formation of an "atheist consciousness" can be seen as a consequence of atheists' heightened awareness of the increasing distance between their strongly held views and the views of the "majority,"[3] which is the result of the diminishing distance due to access to a shared experiential space. In this case an initially limited conflict (e.g., atheist feeling harassed at work) or call to action (e.g., atheist donating money to the cause) is broadened on the basis of an identity and similar interests until it becomes a common affair.

The process of secularists "coming out" and improved means of communication facilitate this unity, creating the space for secularists to emerge and mobilize as a collective group. Consciousness-raising from this perspective "would not be limited to a set of assumptions derived from life experiences that are used to confront, challenge, or resist, from the outside, the dominant ideology" of theism but "could also be conceived as a product of an electronically defined common place that, by virtue of being electronically reproduced, can be considered a public space" (Carpignano et al. 1993: 115–116). This revitalization of atheism and the emergence of a stronger group consciousness and collective identity coincide with the rise of new atheism and the formation of new secularist organizations (especially on college campuses), as well as the reemergence of older organizations with a more public, activist edge. In public, at least, these groups tend to support and refer inquirers to one another.

That feelings of both greater acceptance and exclusion among secularists can emerge from the same dynamics—a simultaneous sense of acceptance and exclusion—helps explain why, on the one hand, most questionnaire respondents felt that prejudice against atheists exists in American society, and, on the other, also reported having raised expectations for the future of secularism. It also helps explain the duality underpinning the secularist ethos today, wherein secularists, in one and the same move, employ the discourse of identity politics based around being a minority while also thinking of and often presenting themselves as a secular vanguard. In *Stigma*, Erving Goffman observes how it can be difficult for minorities to maintain positive self-identities in the face of negative judgment and prejudice from the dominant majorities. In this case of nonbelievers, they are "protected by identity beliefs of [their] own, [they] feel that [they are] full-fledged normal human beings and that [believers] are the ones who are not quite [normal]" (Goffman 1963: 17). Our research confirms this; nonbelievers are embattled yet proud, fearful yet confident. This condition also helps explain why our research found the split personality of secularists concerning their future. The secularization of society functions as a goal at once partially realized, just not fully complete. Far from leading to defeatism or apathy, however, this compels secularists to action, pressing for legal protection of their rights as well as extending their influence through activism. Moreover, the definition of secularism or secularization as the progress of humanity in terms of advances in science and other forms of knowledge and an ever decreasing (and ever more private) role for religion, however difficult to achieve, functions as a "grand narrative of emancipation" (Lyotard 1984) among secularists, both ideologically and politically.

Such a narrative is rooted in science. A recent study found a large subset of secularists with a strongly scientific worldview who were most likely to be drawn to the new atheism (Cragun et al. 2012). Scientific knowledge, in fact, is a major factor in the appeal of secularity, highlighting the notion that the secularist is unique—a rationalist who values truth and has no need for the myths of others; an individual set apart from the norm, misunderstood and misrepresented (especially in the mainstream press)—wherein a divide is established between the scientifically informed, enlightened few and the ignorant religious masses. This idea is reinforced and backed up by notions such as there being a "God gene" (see Zuckerman 2007 for a sociological blow to the "God gene" hypothesis). This is not mentioned to suggest that the psychology of secularity is founded in some form of reactive resentment. It is important, however, to recognize the implicit elitism that often informs secularist vanguardism, especially when one considers that actual revolutions "tend to consist of an alliance between a society's least alienated and its most oppressed" (Graeber 2011: 31). To quote Bill Maher in *Religulous*, "It is a privilege to not have a religion," and far from being a mere genetic defect, religion is also "the expression of real suffering and a protest against real suffering... the sigh of the oppressed creature, the heart of a heartless world, and the soul of soulless conditions" for many people in the world (Marx 1978: 54).

Any authoritative account or perspective of the world is less stable today. If, historically, print helped foster and encourage scientific revolutions and science as a specialized field of knowledge, electronic mediation fosters an environment that challenges such specialization. "New patterns of access to information through electronic media bypass traditional channels and gatekeepers and undermine the pyramids of status that were once supported by print" (Meyrowitz 1985: 163).

Secularists claim the authority of science for themselves in an attempt to "exclude the excluders." However, the mass dispersal of varied discourses made possible by communications technology today makes it harder for a particular discourse, such as a scientific discourse, to claim any a priori primacy. In some respect, the very same conditions that allow for the mass publicizing of an atheistic discourse grounded in science also dilute its potential power to the extent that the line between science and nonscience is more and more blurred, as is apparent in many phenomena today: from self-help literature that draws on popular science to the promotion of creationism and intelligent design as being as scientifically valid as evolution, to the anti-Enlightenment discourses so prevalently promoted under the banner of postmodernism in humanities and social science departments. Incidentally, repercussions of this can even be seen in the new atheist canon itself insofar as the science that informs the arguments are aimed at appealing to an audience beyond the scientific community proper and their academic peers, which inevitably left the authors and the books open to much harsher criticism from such circles than would have likely happened had the arguments been published in peer-reviewed academic journals.

Of course, the work of the Enlightenment is continuing: with the mass dissemination and nonstop blanketing of information, individuals are more capable of examining and researching things for themselves. Intellectual authority has not vanished, but it has lost the power of imposition and become one more opinion up for debate among many. In this, people are not so much invited as demanded to figure things out for themselves and make up their own minds. At the same time, it has become harder to distinguish between information and disinformation: the zaniest and most nonsensical notions and ideas you could ever think up—from conspiracy theories about secret orders running the world to President Obama being a covert Muslim terrorist—are not only welcomed but popular. A respondent to one of our surveys stated this when asked about the possible pros and cons of the Internet for secularists: "The internet is having a positive influence in terms of organization and giving solace to those who live in areas heavily dominated by religion. It may also have positive effects in terms of education, but I do see quite a bit of uncritical acceptance on atheists' part in terms of accepting some ahistorical statements to back their arguments, e.g. using Graves' '16 Crucified Saviors' to back the Jesus myth hypothesis, and claiming that the Council of Nicaea voted on the books to be included in the Bible." And, as another atheist stated, "It will advance rational thought, but irrational thought as well—holocaust deniers, conspiracy theorists, hate groups, etc. that would not otherwise have much [of a] voice."

We focus more fully on the Internet in the next chapter. For now, though, the increased visibility and awareness, which are inseparable from new forms of experience and publicity arising from the expansion of the communicative conditions of contemporary media in general (and not just online), both express and broaden the scope of American secularists' participation in society. Such an expansion is especially significant for secularists in terms of equality of cultural creation and participating in constructing messages and representing themselves, since their public image has more often been constructed by others. But tensions remain among secularists about the best way to promote the cause. The spectrum in such debates run the gamut, from those who promote a notion of publicity premised more on formal means of communication (deliberation, polite argument) to those favoring less formal and more personal notions of publicity based more on their own personal experience and everyday lives. One reason that more vocal atheists face such opposition in the United States is related not only to the fact that they challenge religious belief, but also to the fact that they challenge the communicative and democratic norm of neutrality when it comes to matters of faith.

Bringing different views about the new atheism and the proper way to promote the secular cause to the fore, we found a segment of secularists arguing—in both the content of *Free Inquiry* and, to a lesser extent, the *American Atheist* and in the responses to our questionnaire—that the new atheists are too openly hostile to religion, while others feel that a total critique of religion is long overdue. As one respondent said, "I think such 'nasty attitudes' are self-defeating. Achieving atheism is a matter that requires much thought, with as little extraneous noise as possible." In contrast, another stated, "I refuse to distinguish myself from the New Atheism. Religion ... deserves to be harshly criticized." Attractive cultural symbols or messages do not always get produced and emanate from the center. Sometimes they come from the periphery. In fact, one way to understand the success of new atheism is to say that it was an outsider position becoming popular, or a marginal cultural production successfully moving toward the center.

Ironically, partly because of the increased visibility due to the success of the books and the enthusiasm generated among atheists, some secularists now find themselves on the defensive. Greg Epstein (2009a), for example, has used the publicity generated around the new atheists to promote humanism—or the "new new atheism" as he calls it—as a positive alternative to atheism that "seeks to... actually build coalitions with religious people of all stripes around important issues." In the same way, Paul Kurtz used the opportunity to reiterate his longtime distinction between secular humanism and atheism, stating that "for the secular humanist, it is not so much the stridency of these books that is at issue, as it is what's missing from these books."[4] Epstein and Kurtz argued that what is missing from this uncompromising critique of religion is the affirmation of ethical values, humanistic virtues, and democratic principles.[5] Another respondent from our survey said as much: "I do think that advocating an anti position is a disadvantage. I prefer that we speak of what we value in positive terms: reason, scientific inquiry, separation of church and state. I do not want to be seen as a nihilist."

The dilemma for the more mainstream and moderate secularists, such as Kurtz and Epstein, is the concern that some of the more publicly outspoken secularists are offering the general public a partial and distorted image of secularism, a concern that has increased with the heterogeneity of secularist voices and perspectives coming out online. Moderates see little advantage in the cacophony of voices and perspectives, with some arguing that such activity is doing more harm than good and actually multiplying misunderstandings.

At the other end of the spectrum are "militant" atheists, such as PZ Myers, who promote and prioritize the virtues of a highly personalized and aggressive mode of atheism set against the perceived weaknesses of a more accommodating atheism. These conflicting views over the best approaches to proclaiming atheism and consciousness-raising echo the long-standing, if renewed and now more public, division between those secularists who start with attacking religion and those secularists who start from a more live-and-let-live position toward religion and promote a positive system of secular ethics as a first step, in the manner of Kurtz and Epstein. Of course, although we are using the extreme example of new atheism versus humanism for our comparisons, it is more appropriate to view secularist stances on any issue along a continuum and to view moderates and hard-liners as ideal types (a point we return to below). In this instance, even the most extreme anti-accommodationist, militant atheists would have an ethics they view as positive and also have humanistic impulses, insofar as destroying religion in their eyes is for the betterment of humanity.

While moderates are correct in being worried about the problem of controlling images in our hyper-mediated age, the idea that the representation of secularists and secularity is more distorted today than in the past should be challenged. In fact, to the extent that more secularists than ever are going public *as themselves* and seeking change on their own personal terms—as opposed to being represented in the press, or having organizations speaking on their behalf—we might actually argue that the image of secularists and secularity is far less distorted today, precisely due to so many partial, personal perspectives becoming public.

Overall, insiders and outsiders alike should be cautious about drawing the conclusion that the new atheist phenomenon is having a negative impact. Internal debates are part and parcel of more secularist voices coming to the fore, not necessarily evidence of fragmentation. In other words, that there is more internal debate taking place in public today is not necessarily evidence that internal debate is any more frequent today than in the past, only evidence that it is more visible. Moreover, such debates are consistent with our political system and the assumption that in any dynamic society there would and should be contending interest groups in perpetual debate, deliberation, and conflict playing off one another—a notion that informs the separation of powers. Additionally, underrepresented groups often pursue quite different strategies of action than other, more privileged groups. These actions, such as aesthetic gestures, musical protests, rallies, and demonstrations, do not conform to rational discourse aimed at a consensus but can nonetheless be seen as legitimate on their own terms. Such actions can be understood not so much as being defensive as being dynamic expressions actively aimed at changing the social order. Also, some analysts assert that a big part of the newness of new atheism has as much, if not more, to do with its commercial and media appeal than anything substantively new philosophically.

Strategically, this diversity and internal dissent could be an advantage to the secularist movement. As a respondent to our survey put it, "I wish people would stop fostering the perception that secularists are [seriously at] odds with each other over semantics and approaches.... Sure, secularists have different approaches to furthering the same causes, but the different approaches seem to be effective under different circumstances. It seems that Epstein and 'the new atheists' appreciate each other's work despite any disagreements."

According to Joshua Meyrowitz, integrating all groups into a relatively common sphere with a common set of options does not lead to homogenization but to "the development of many new, more superficial, more shifting groupings that form against the now relatively unified backdrop of common information":

> People traditionally united and divided into groups that corresponded primarily to social class, ethnicity, race, education type and level, religion, occupation, and neighborhood. But current groupings also develop on the basis of wearing similar clothes, participating in similar sports, listening to the same type of music, or attending the same class. (Meyrowitz 1994: 69)

One could add to the list reading the same books. Our research consistently indicated the centrality of the new atheist books for secularists. Thus, however one may characterize it—or criticize and depreciate the books and their authors—the new atheist phenomenon is still arguably the single most important and influential event shaping contemporary secularity today. Many of our respondents, for example, noted the powerful and important influence the books and authors had on both their atheist identity and activism. In response to a question asking how the books have informed their secularity, for instance, some simply stated that they "have become more comfortable and open about [their] atheism." "It has made me prouder to be an atheist!" exclaimed one. Others highlighted how they "don't feel alone anymore, even [though] within [their] personal circles there's still not a lot of [support]." One respondent elaborated by noting how the books and atheists coming out "help to expose a hidden constituency that can be powerful and influential." The influential texts were also referred to in the context of raising awareness, with many noting how, in the words of one respondent, "these famous authors' books broadened [their] understanding of why religions are so dangerous in the 21st Century." Another "now [sees] the tragic consequences of religious beliefs throughout history and to this day." One simply concluded, "I have been radicalized."

The general consensus was that the various authors and books provide "alternative perspectives" and "blend into a full spectrum approach to understanding the complexities of atheism." This broad, full-spectrum approach is important for contemporary secularity. The secularist landscape is highly pluralistic, with multiple subgroups or "minor publics" (forming against a relatively unified backdrop) made up of highly individualistic people holding diverse philosophies. What makes this diversity a dilemma for the broader secularist movement is the hurdle for consensus it presents. If secularist organizations, groups, and individuals disagree on the fundamentals, how can they be expected to unify and cooperate, especially when one considers that such a high percentage of secularists are not formally affiliated with any secular organization and consider the whole notion of a secularist community, movement, or political party completely unnecessary, if not downright un-secularist-like, given the high priority placed on being autonomous in being and thought?

While such questions cannot be answered definitely here, we can make a few points. First, all the recent research suggests that the potential for a collective political front is rapidly becoming a reality. Second, secularist identity politics is rooted in ideology and ideas instead of gender, ethnicity, race, or religion. As such, disagreements are easier to both start and tolerate, being about differences in opinions and ideas as opposed to deep-seated belief systems or traditions (backed by a powerful institutional or organizational apparatus that determines who belongs and who doesn't) or unchangeable differences as a matter of birth, origin, or nationality. Further, secularist identity politics are largely based on various readings of science, and science as a field and a practice must necessarily remain open to criticism and new evidence to a degree that other fields and practices do not. This necessity informs certain aspects of contemporary secularity irrespective of whether particular secularist readings of the scientific literature are biased, ideologically laden, or "closed." Finally, and returning to the first point, such diversity can be a benefit, a point made more than once by our respondents as well as in the texts we reviewed.

Modern secularity often defines itself in opposition to traditional forms of belonging, specifically to institutional forms that appear churchlike. In opposition to learning sacred texts and dogmatic formulas, secularists seek to draw selectively on a variety of sources to construct and craft their own particular identities and meaning, which is one reason that secularist self-identities and groups are so varied. In this respect, contemporary secularity reflects broader trends in society, specifically the decline in traditional patterns of belonging to formal institutions. This situation is equally the result and cause of the rise of nones and secularity more broadly.

In contrast to strict organizational forms that have trouble accommodating too much heterogeneity without fracturing, the horizontal lightness of secularist forms of organizing allows for greater inclusiveness in spite of differences among individual participants. Such lightness can also accommodate and allow for more iconoclastic, innovative, and radical cultural productions (a point we look at again in the next chapter). Similarly, compared with strict identity or cultural commitments, the weak and loose commitments among secularists open them up to a wider collectivity than is possible on the basis of strong commitments; weak ties, as opposed to the strong ties that form among small groups of individuals, allow a greater and more rapid spreading of information across not only geographic distances but class, gender, racial, and ethnic divisions as well (Granovetter 1973; Meyrowitz 1994)—affirming an emergent movement that is informationally greater than the sum of its participants. Connecting such individuals and constituting this space enables secularists to set aside other roles and responsibilities and enter the public sphere with their secularity as their primary and true identity and selves. This, in turn, gives shape and form to an imagined community in the minds of participants, allowing them over time and increased exposure to form denser cognitive associations and a more robust collective identity.

To give an example, consider the job of a professor like PZ Myers. When teaching, his atheism takes a back seat to the material he is required to teach. However, when writing as a public intellectual on his blog, he writes first and foremost as an atheist—and his goals change accordingly. These posts bring about a variety of readers and responses; for instance, one person may comment positively on a post while another may disagree with a finer point. Yet another may link the article to his or her own site or like the post on Facebook, or even write a full post in response, while another may only visit and read without responding. Through participation in these activities, secularists may revise their ideas, their knowledge of certain issues may be reaffirmed or enhanced, or they may feel a greater desire to take action and participate in offline activism. In repeating such actions and engaging in such activities, their identity and the larger secularist network it reproduces are continuously influenced and reshaped in various ways.

The circulation of atheist ideas and ideologies has increased exponentially. Greater visibility has opened up the opportunity for secularists whose politics, philosophies, life experiences, and social statuses differ to acknowledge one another and join together on the basis of what they share. The new atheist books are a distinctive and important part of this phenomenon. The impact of this phenomenon is all the more significant and impressive given that the U.S. political discourse and the popular media that nourishes and feeds on it is still fundamentally sympathetic to religious interests rhetorically and, by extension, in large measure hostile to the notion of nonbelief and nonbelievers as a group. Indeed, in accessing American attitudes since O'Hair's media presence, it is apparent that the modern new atheist discourse, driven by Dawkins et al., has provided the main—if not the only—challenge to the remaining norms of American religiosity that still exist—if often latently so more than manifestly so—whenever atheism is discussed or covered in the mainstream media and press (see Goldberg 2009).

The long-standing and still often prevailing stereotype and image of atheists as angry and antisocial has not been effaced, and indeed has been reinforced in some ways with the increased publicity and the conflation of all atheists with the most confrontational voices in the court of public opinion.

And while massive misunderstandings persist, with the very word "atheist" still striking a mix of fear and subversion in many rural, highly religious regions in the United States, the phenomenon of the new atheism has undoubtedly done more than any other recent event in American secularist history to (1) give nonbelievers a public voice; (2) provide nonbelievers a general canon with which to unify, dissent, and, most importantly, communicate with one another; and (3) express an oppositional alternative ethos in which sacred institutions are criticized. The new atheism offers a meta-critique of religion that is unique in putting forth the argument that even moderate religiosity is deeply implicated in the moral catastrophes perpetuated on the world in the name of religion, insofar as they implicitly provide support and cover for religious extremists (to the extent that moderates use and defend the same resources, materials, and beliefs that extremists use to justify their actions and causes).

Thus, although the books have been criticized quite strongly by scholars and experts, what such critics miss is the function and role they play. Taken collectively, the books represent a vernacular in which a diverse and potentially global (some of the books have been widely translated) population of secularists may invent and imagine their identities, narratives, and traditions. The accusations about the new atheism being mean-spirited, militant, aggressive, and even counterproductive may well ring true for those outside the secularist fold, but it is also the case that what "is conceived as a confrontational device becomes an opening for the empowerment of an alternative discursive practice. These [unabashedly antireligious discourses] don't have to conform to civility nor to the dictates of the general interest. They can be expressed for what they are: particular, regional, one-sided, and for that reason politically alive" (Carpignano et al. 1993: 116).

Chapter 3

Atheisms Unbound
*Moving Toward the Center, Speaking
from the Margins*

The world's largest atheist community is not found in any building
or city, yet it serves as both a refuge for beleaguered secularists and a
launching pad for attacks against religion and broadsides for atheist
rights. With close to 2 million subscribers, this atheist community
is just a click away on the social and entertainment website Reddit.
According to its many testimonial posts, the forum, known as /r/
atheism, is a lifeboat in a sea of religious intolerance and incredulity.
It provides instructions on how to come out as an atheist and even
offers atheist havens—members' homes where newly minted atheists can crash to find support if they have been disowned by their
families for their disbelief. As one poster commented:

> One week ago I worshiped the Bible. One week ago I wasted
> Sundays mornings at church. One week ago I was convinced in
> a fairy tale. One week ago I believed in a talking burning bush?
> (don't ask why). One week ago I was clueless, but then all or a
> sudden /r/atheism!!! You guys have made me see clearly from
> the moment I started an account. I first found this forum when
> a friend of mine sent me a link; he said "this site will cure you of
> all your sins," so of course I went for it. It led me to /r/atheism.

Since /r/atheism is one of the largest communities on Reddit, far bigger than any religious forums, it begs the question of whether the Internet and secularism share some affinity. In fact, the secularist presence is found on many websites and blogs promoting, discussing, referencing, reflecting on, and critiquing atheism. In this chapter we argue that such sites have opened up an active space for atheists to construct and share mutual concerns about their situation at a time when American public life is still functioning under a norm of religiosity in many contexts. These websites, Facebook pages, Twitter posts, and other forums function as public spaces by virtue of being electronically reproduced and disseminated, and they have become important components of atheist activism, especially in terms of information distribution and consciousness-raising. Only in grasping the inherently public and connected medium of the Internet can the matrix of atheist interactions online rightly be considered collective and viewed as a form of activism. Of course, as we have seen throughout this book, atheist activism can mean many things, expressed in quite different strains of secularism. Just as the Internet is based on a model of narrowcasting against a backdrop of broadcasting, this medium reveals a plurality of smaller identity groupings within a larger, general, and increasingly global secularist collective.

The Internet has facilitated a more visible and active secular identity, which we consider a form of activism in terms of promoting the importance of secularist concerns and issues in public discourse. But what is the relationship between secularist cyber-activism and secular organizations, or between secularist activism and U.S. politics in general? Answering these questions helps us to further underscore the importance of the Internet for contemporary secularism, since it helps develop and reflects a collective identity based around broadly similar agendas and ideas that are both cause and effect of secularists' greater motivation and mobilization, online as well as offline.

As we discussed in the last chapter, the popular and highly successful new atheist presence in print has opened up a legitimate market for secularist thought. Of course, secularists, like most everyone else, often seek out books, information, and similarly minded people to confirm rather than challenge their beliefs and ideals (Nickerson 1998; Kunda 1999; Oswald and Grosjean 2004)—behavior that the Internet potentially exacerbates with the ability to close down comments and police sites in ways that are counterproductive to serious debate and discussions. This in effect creates an in-group for a particular strand of thought or philosophy. Determining whether exposure to or availability of such books and information has led individuals to "deconvert" from their religions is beyond the scope of this book, but what can be confirmed is that the Internet has allowed for a quantitative leap in the amount and range of material available. Starting with "African Americans for Humanism" and ending with "Young Freethought," the link pages on the website of the Richard Dawkins Foundation (www.richarddawkins.net) list about 150 secularist websites. Also available are a number of group-oriented blogs and forums as well as the scattered array of videos and podcasts, and even Facebook groups. In short, one finds a vast assortment of media and various cultural productions made by and for a specialized atheist and secular audience, creating an atheist popular culture of sorts. Individual atheists in America seeking out explicitly pro-atheist messages in print who used to have to look to organizational newsletters or perhaps the occasional article in a publication now have numerous sources at their fingertips. Similarly, atheist organizations and activists who used to struggle for greater recognition and were almost entirely ignored by the mainstream media now know that almost any event or rally they hold will be reported on and covered by someone somewhere—if only on a forum visited by other atheists. This uptick in coverage and cultural production, coupled and associated with growing commercial success, has also influenced the mainstream media's treatment of atheism.

ATHEISTS AND THE OLD AND NEW MEDIA

Already by the early 2000s a marked change had taken place from only two decades earlier in how atheists were represented and featured in much of the media. While conservative critics regularly attacked such newspapers as the *Washington Post* and the *New York Times* for being bastions of liberal secularism, the representation of atheist views and the reporting of atheist activity had both been limited and low-key since the nineteenth century. The *New York Times* has shifted its coverage of atheism from being that of a Christian heresy to an independent social movement with its own identity and culture. Atheist deliberations and activism have moved mainstream media toward more favorable treatment of this group, on the one hand, while also exposing atheists to further misunderstanding and opposition, on the other.[1]

In the early part of twentieth century, the *Times'* coverage of atheism tended to be framed by nationwide controversies over theological liberalism in mainline Protestant churches, which critics often conflated with unbelief and atheism. Religious leaders often cited atheism as a source of constant danger that believers might fall into, and their warnings were reported as an opportunity for recommitment to the faith. Atheism continued to be covered as a foil for Christianity up until the 1960s. Under the influence of the Cold War, the atheistic aspects of communism had received new attention, but it was the more coordinated attempts to challenge the role of religion in public life that most often brought atheism to the public's attention. Madalyn Murray O'Hair and her successful crusade to remove prayer from the public schools in 1963 diverted the attention of the media from other secularist groups. By the late 1960s, however, atheism was more frequently portrayed apart from a critical or antagonistic religious context and covered on its own merits, increasingly by religion writers. But such coverage was still infrequent and framed around church-state issues, largely because of O'Hair's visibility in comparison with other atheist-freethought groups.

In the 1970s, news outlets started to pay attention to the growing diversity in organized atheist ranks; O'Hair also played a role in this change, but it was mainly because of unrest and dissent within her group, American Atheists. The coverage of these schisms was similar in tone and style to reports of any religious denomination suffering from conflict and scandals. Coverage in the first decade of the millennium broadened to include atheism as a lifestyle and a personal and political identity as well as a movement. The fact that some *Times* editors and writers publicly identified with atheism was a drastic change from just three decades earlier. In a 2001 article titled "Confessions of a Lonely Atheist," *Times* science writer Natalie Angier reviewed the still-prevalent animosity toward atheism in the United States at a time when public religiosity was prevalent, and then outed herself as an atheist (Angier 2001). In counterpoint to the growing influence of the Christian right, several articles also reported on the growing outspokenness of atheists. In another article, religion reporter Laurie Goodstein (2009) reported how atheists and secular humanists in South Carolina, as well as in the nation as a whole, were growing and networking as they sought to counteract the influence of the religious right.

The *Times* also noticed the rise of the new atheism. Most of this coverage was critical, with religion columnist Peter Steinfels critiquing the "dogmatism" of new atheist authors, reflecting the narrow stance of their religious antagonists and even the precarious state of the Enlightenment in meeting current challenges.[2] Steinfels and other writers seemed to reflect a general stance of the *Times* and other elite newspapers of portraying the new atheists as too negative and critical about religion. Perhaps the aggressive attacks on religion launched by the new atheists were deemed too radical for a newspaper that itself editorialized against the public role of religious institutions on such issues as abortion, gay rights, and politics in general. Traditionally, the *Times* draws on liberal and moderate religious allies in its stance favoring a limited role for religion in politics—a strategy that would be endangered by associating itself with the new atheism and its antagonism for religion in general, whether liberal, moderate, or conservative.

Yet for all the distance between the media and the new atheism, the phenomenon did make atheism more visible. In our examination of *Washington Post* articles on atheism between 1989 and 2013, there was a significant difference in the style of reporting before and after 2006 (when most of the new atheist books were published and the phenomenon was first dubbed the "new atheism"). First, there was an expansion of coverage: of the 150 articles examined, about two-thirds were published in 2006 and after. But the tone and style of the reportage and commentary stood out the most. Pre-2006 articles tended to fall into the categories of church-state issues (reporting on atheist activism for stricter separation of church and state), events and incidents involving O'Hair or her successors, and the events of September 11, 2001, which ignited coverage of atheist attacks against religion. Most of these articles were hard news stories with little color in the way of personality profiles or first-person narratives.

The post-2006 articles were similar to those of the *New York Times* in the same period: coverage of atheist diversity beyond O'Hair and her successors. Stories explored not only a variety of organizations but also the ways atheism was integrated into individuals' everyday lives, dealing with family and identity issues. Coverage included a feature on an atheist camp, reporting on atheist parenting in the face of tragedies, stories on how atheists handle holidays, and an article on the innovation of "kosher atheism." For all the quantitative increase in coverage and qualitative change in tone, mainstream media coverage of atheism remains problematic.

One issue is that the media tend to follow a limited number of scripts and focus on conventional or sensational themes that preclude in-depth treatment and serious discussion. For example, stories in media coverage often paint atheists as aggressive and belligerent, despite the fact that most atheist activism is no more or less aggressive than any other democratically abiding activism (as opposed to illiberal hate groups that fail and have no intention to abide by democratic procedures). In fact, when you strip away the rhetoric that the mass media and critics alike are so prone to latch on to, the activism and message of the new atheism are firmly consistent with our democratic principles and procedures inherited from thinkers such as John Stuart Mill, specifically his argument for freedom of speech and the Enlightenment notion that all authoritative statements should not only be allowed but tested by means of an open, public use of debate and reason.[3] Without adequate and accurate coverage, however, atheists appear in the media as a brash, unorganized group, which keeps them distant and distinct from the American mainstream. Mark Silk's study of the press's use of religious topoi also helps explain the tendency to focus on conventional themes that preclude in-depth treatment of the philosophical and religious questions surrounding the new atheism. Silk (1995) finds that the media follow a limited number of storylines or topoi that include such religious and quasi-religious values as tolerance, inclusiveness, opposition to hypocrisy, "good works," exposing "false prophets" and unconventional religions, and even a sympathy (at least in tabloids and newsweeklies) for the supernatural. Such a repertoire applied toward atheism might limit the media's sensitivity toward secularist issues and provide animus toward such a contentious phenomenon as the new atheism. At the same time, however, these storylines of inclusiveness and tolerance are broad enough to reach outside of mainstream religion to include atheism, at least in its gentler forms.

Our Internet survey of atheists found similar tensions in their views of the media. For example, when asked, "Do you feel that the media—particularly popular media—is supportive of your secularism/atheism?" one respondent answered, "I do feel that the media takes a fairly open view of beliefs . . . although biased 'reporters' such as Glenn Beck and Bill O'Reilly make things difficult with their bigoted attempts to turn all things un-Christian into evil incarnate in the public eye." Another stated that the media provide "mixed support depending on the conservative/liberal bias of the media source."

On the one hand, mainstream newspapers and professional journalism are understood as neutral forums for public debate; on the other, they are understood as partisan and biased. Understanding these contradictory and overlapping views of the press and media more generally helps explain the ambivalence as well as the growing discontent with "the media," or a crisis of legitimacy of the news as a social institution, especially among minority groups such as atheists. "Atheism has always been cast in the lowest regard by the media and most everyone in America," asserted one atheist surveyed. "I tend to be more outspoken now."

In considering this last quote, one role that the mainstream media and press may play in the formation of a sense of community among a dispersed population of atheists is that of excluding them from the dominant discourse, and thus articulating their outsider status and pushing them to form a counterpublic with one another. The term "counterpublic" signifies, first, that not all significant speech occurs in officially sanctioned manners or forums, and second, that there are always multiple publics and varied forms of publicity operating within a general or more dominant notion of "the public." In perceiving themselves to be excluded and communicating about it, they help constitute a discursive arena. This communication may take place in physical spaces, but it may also take place through dispersed, asynchronous communication online. We now turn to the latter.

SECULARISTS MOBILIZING AND COUNTERMOBILIZING ONLINE

Blogs and YouTube videos have become an important part of secularist culture and activism. They promote a highly personalized mode of presentation. A no-holds-barred style, such as that found on a blog like PZ Myers's highly popular Pharyngula, appeals to secularists because of the uncompromising opinions and views it expresses. Readers—many of whom comment on posts—are not so much interested in getting an objective view of an issue or news item when they visit Pharyngula; they want Myers's singular, iconoclastic take on whatever particular subject he tackles. As a site for Myers to promote his particular brand of atheism, often dubbed "militant" by himself and others, Pharyngula functions as a secularist source of information set against not only the perceived deficiencies of the mainstream press but also against the accommodating tendencies of more moderate forms of atheism. In a post from April 2010 titled "Witless Wanker Peddles Pablum for CFI," for example, Myers castigates the secular humanist Center for Inquiry's Michael De Dora for his "willingness to accommodate *any* nonsense from religious BS artists." In response, Massimo Pigliucci of the blog "Rationally Speaking" wrote a post (2010a) titled "PZ Myers Is a Witless Wanker Who Peddles Pablum." In the piece Pigliucci criticizes Myers's post for being "the latest example of an escalation (downwards in quality) in the tone and substance of the discourse on atheism," which he blames "broadly on the rhetoric of the new atheism (the only 'new' aspect of which is precisely the in-your-face approach to 'reason')." Pigliucci, opting for a more restrained approach, thinks Myers's and the other new atheists' rhetoric casts atheism in a bad light, whereas the new atheists understand that well-publicized transgressions against norms can embolden an audience.

From one perspective, Myers's and Pigliucci's posts merely reflect the long-standing divisions that exist between those atheists content to attack religion and other, more conciliatory atheists concerned with promoting a positive system of secular ethics. In studying the links between secularist websites, we also found similar divisions, with atheist sites and blogs regularly linking to each other but not necessarily to secular humanist groups such as CFI, while other groups that disassociate themselves from the atheist label and seek to promote a new secularist identity, such as the "brights," tend not to link to other sites at all. From another perspective, these posts highlight some very real differences regarding attitudes among atheists, specifically relating to public debate and views of science. For Pigliucci, as we can see in his critique of Myers and the new atheists, public discourse should be oriented toward and proceed in a rational and civil manner, even when seeking to critique another. Myers, on the other hand, goes in for a take-no-prisoners approach, eschewing any posturing toward neutrality and civility when expressing himself as an atheist. Myers's individualistic stance points to another factor underpinning the disagreement. On his blog, Myers is speaking as a singular atheist, not as a professor tied to an institution. Pigliucci's blog, on the other hand, has strong links to CFI. While we don't think this point should be overemphasized—since Pigliucci is not speaking solely on behalf of CFI—it also shouldn't be completely ignored. As we see in the concluding section of the chapter, a big difference exists in how organizations and independents seek to appeal to the public—so much so, in fact, that we might say they are addressing different publics.

Another disagreement has to do with their view of science. Pigliucci, holding to a more modest view of science, defends the modernist notion that differences between fields should be respected, arguing that properly philosophical and religious questions should not, and ultimately cannot, be answered by scientific inquiry. New atheists like Myers, in contrast, promote the view that there are virtually no limits to science and that the burden of proof lies with those who insist on denying such scientific progress and those who presume to dismiss the attempt of science to explain the currently unexplained as impossible in principle. In their view, scientific progress, and progress in general, has progressed in spite of religion, never because of it.

All of this suggests patterns of mobilization and countermobilization as well as internal boundary marking (Gamson 1997), as secular activists and secularist organizations seek to distinguish and promote their particular brand of secular activism or organization from others within the same milieu or movement, even as new bonds and alliances form and a greater unity is emerging. Such boundary marking is directly related to the influx of diverse participants sharing the same space and can be observed on various forums.

A large and decentralized venue such as Reddit's /r/atheism forum, for example, has served to publicize smaller atheist blogs and websites to a larger audience and create more intergroup unity. Dave Muscato of American Atheists, for instance, praises /r/atheism for linking to the small blog he wrote for the Secular Students Alliance, not only for promoting and publicizing this fast-growing group on college campuses, but also for creating the contacts to help him gain a full-time position with American Atheists (Muscato 2013). At the same time, we can see how such venues—and the autonomy and lack of responsibility they enable—can bring certain underlying schisms within the movement (which would remain in the background within a more formalized setting) to the front stage. Recently, for example, a fifteen-year-old girl was subjected to sexual harassment on Reddit. The incident, which has become known as "redditgate" (Miller 2013), occurred after the teen posted a picture of herself holding a book she received for Christmas from her "super-religious mother"; she then started receiving sexually explicit comments based on her photograph. This harassment is not limited to cyberspace.

A piece published by the Religion News Service explored the accusations of women claiming they had been subjected to unwanted advances and harassment at The Amazing Meeting (TAM) and other atheist and skeptic events (Winston 2012). Rebecca Watson, a prominent skeptic blogger who was slated to speak at TAM, went so far as to cancel her presentation on account of not feeling "safe." In response to Watson's resignation, TAM's organizer, D. J. Grothe, spoke out, stating that he wished the people would find some common ground between the negative reports and the efforts that are being made to assure that all women feel welcome.

At the World Atheist Conference the year before, Watson was involved in another controversy, claiming she was approached by a man in an elevator who she believed was wanting sex. After posting a video online explaining what happened—an incident that has come to be know as "elevatorgate" (see Freethought Kampala 2011 for an overview)—the blogosphere went ablaze with a blog war between those siding with Watson and those critical of her, including other female atheists. Richard Dawkins, chiming in on the debate, responded with the cutting remark that Watson should "grow a thicker skin."[4]

As the redditgate and elevatorgate incidents clearly show, anonymity online can be a double-edged sword. On one hand, such anonymity allows those who may be fearful or shy the opportunity to express themselves, which is especially important for individuals or groups that may face a certain amount of discrimination or a stigma in their family or local community. Along with this, all those social markers—class, race, religion, gender, and so on—that strongly impact and influence who can say what to whom and where in face-to-face communication are largely absent. On the other hand, a sense of irresponsibility often accompanies such anonymity online; there is often no consequence for a person acting irrationally or hatefully toward another. The worst punishment a person may receive is being banned from wherever they were causing trouble, but it does not banish them from making other remarks on another website or under another name. The balance between responsibility and anonymity largely depends on the goal and the discourse sought. "I definitely think it helps to have a meeting place with like-minded folks," said a female atheist we surveyed. "Since we are still a fairly small and quiet part of the populace, it's especially nice to be able speak freely on the web. I know that where I'm rather shy about announcing myself as an atheist generally, I'm able to find community there—so it's a very good resource. The only negative aspect, as with all groups, is the antagonists, people who are probably normal in life, but for some reason become crazy when they feel the protection of the anonymous internet."

If the goal is to sexually harass or spread hate speech, then anonymity loses its role as a security measure. If, on the other hand, the goal is to provide political opposition or criticism, then such anonymity can be harnessed for activism in terms of public awareness and advocacy, especially when the opposing positions and opinions are expressed in a confrontational fashion.

Atheist Revolution's vjack and Austin Cline (who writes about atheism on about.com) defend mockery (vjack 2011) and assertiveness (Cline 2010) as necessary atheist strategies. As Cline, whom vjack quotes in his post, writes,

> The sad fact is, atheists were not getting positive press and love from the general public *before* the so-called "new atheists" and their more assertive tactics appeared. Being less assertive and more submissive is no way to promote change and there's absolutely no reason to think that it would make the situation for atheists in America any better.

Myers's inflammatory views or assertive tactics, such as mockery, would likely never be published in a mainstream media outlet. Online, however, this is not the case. The Internet allows individuals only weakly tied through information distribution networks to inadvertently collaborate in the dissemination of ideas and advance certain issues without sacrificing their individual autonomy and identity for the greater good of an organization or movement (a point we discuss further below). In institutionalized activism, on the other hand, varying actors and identities are required to compete for representation, often requiring a reduction of the multiple issues and identities at stake.

YouTube's old slogan, "Broadcast Yourself," sounds like an oxymoron. Broadcasting has traditionally been associated with a privileged few, namely large media organizations. The individual secularists who put up videos cannot be said to be formally collaborating with one another on the YouTube site; the relations between these various videos and the individuals who post them on their channel are too indirect. Instead of speaking to one another directly, the secularists posting videos are likely to be discussing and debating particular issues that are important to them personally, presenting their own personal and singular views on a given subject. Thunderf00t and The Amazing Atheist's videos are good examples of this, with the former's popular video series *Why People Laugh at Creationists* seeking to show the foolishness of creationism and intelligent design by juxtaposing clips of creationists and other religious conservatives. The substance and tone of Thunderf00t's videos are that of the professional, well-educated, and articulate British academic expert exposing—in voiceover—the irrational behavior and attitudes of the believer. In contrast, The Amazing Atheist takes up the role of the informed and entertaining everyman. Spanning a broad spectrum of subjects, many of these videos cover current events and issues, which, along with the comedic aspect, perhaps broaden the ability to reach beyond the deconverted. The Amazing Atheist presents his views and arguments with a mix of humor and vitriol.

In the course of debating, debunking, and critiquing other YouTubers, such as pro-creationist VenomFangX and libertarian HowTheWorldWorks, Thunderf00t and The Amazing Atheist have both taken advantage of the fair-use clause in U.S. copyright law, which allows users to legally use segments of other's videos in their own. These exchanges and borrowings also highlight "one of the current pitfalls of U.S. Copyright law: the application of the Digital Millennium Copyright Act (DMCA) Takedown Notices. This is a clause in the DMCA under which copyright owners who believe their work is being infringed upon (beyond fair use) via the Internet can merely notify the carrier to remove the material" (Farley 2009). Such a clause has allowed opponents, who in this instance are mostly pro-creationists, to file false charges against secularists, the most infamous being the false claims issued by VenomFangX against some of Thunderf00t's videos. To combat such abuses, individual secularists filed counterclaims and spoke out against the abuse in their individual videos. Such countermobilization resulted in a group of secularist users, including Thunderf00t, forming a "multi-national alliance." This alliance set up a channel called DMCAabuse and created a video titled "Creationist DMCA abuse" (DMCAabuse 2008). They also drafted a statement that read, in part,

> We all share an interest in science and we have respect for the advancements and benefits that science has brought us. The Internet is one example of this. We believe that the internet offers extraordinary and valuable opportunities for education, and through sites such as you tube, a forum for open discussion and exchange of views. In order for people to fully benefit from the Internet, freedom of speech, freedom of expression and a lack of censorship are essential. (DMCAabuse 2008)

This effort suggests the potential of the Internet for outreach and collective action. As Tim Farley, discussing YouTube and the skeptical movement, confirms,

> YouTube is an excellent avenue for skeptical outreach on the Internet. Its ease of use and lack of fees lower the barrier of entry

so almost any skeptic can participate. Fair use ensures a steady stream of source material to debunk. The high traffic of the site and its explorability make the skeptical message accessible to people who may not even be aware of organized skepticism. Any skeptic with minimal audiovisual editing skills should consider YouTube an outlet for their efforts. (Farley 2009)

Such efforts in using the Internet for outreach and collective action also demonstrate how secularist efforts are capable of springing up from below, in the moment, as the need or issue arises, without representational mechanisms, institutions, or organizations that might seek to determine or steer such collective action.

Almost every atheist we interviewed and surveyed acknowledged the benefits of the Internet in terms of outreach and community building, specifically for those atheists isolated in the religious hinterlands. One respondent who is active in NYC Atheists, hosts the cable TV show *Atheist History Week*, and is president (and the newsletter editor) of the Secular Humanist Society of New York, expressed similar sentiments:

The Internet is having a positive effect because it allows people to "meet" others with the same points of view—this is especially true (and positive) in small town and Bible belt areas where people are often afraid to voice their atheist or a-religious feelings. Whether that translates into activism or real education is still an open-ended question. As in many other political/social areas, people think watching a video on YouTube is activism, i.e.: "I learned the song. I bought the t-shirt. I'm done."

These responses highlight the positive attributes that the expansion of communicative technologies play in terms of opening up associational spaces for atheists to connect, and they also highlight the dilemmas, trade-offs, and multiple purposes that often accompany such connections and technology.

SECULARIST WEAK TIES AND "SOFT ACTIVISM": HOW SECULARIST MEDIA IS DRIVING A NEW SOCIAL MOVEMENT

As our sample of blogs and videos attests, atheists, like many underrepresented groups, are not content to merely be represented by others today; they desire to present themselves and speak out on their own behalf. This desire to self-represent is intensified with atheists appearing in the center of a picture that they themselves would like to produce—a picture or representation that, paradoxically, also constitutes a common space. As stated previously, the Internet not only transmits information and representations to a public but also functions as a source of publicity or presentation itself insofar as being public today increasingly means being online. Part of the Internet's power and appeal for historically underrepresented groups is that it provides them with the material means to speak out "in public, as themselves, unscripted and unrehearsed, as writers of their own texts and producers of their own public pronouncements and utterances.... Such discursive practices represent an unprecedented intrusion of [atheists] into the discursive apparatus of the media. And this intrusion accounts, to a great degree, for the very visible shift in the direction of the private, the intimate, in public debate" (Carpignano 1999: 187).

Social media gives private issues and concerns a more public airing. What happens online, in the private and personal domain of secularists, is potentially infused with public meaning. The power that makes up much of formal life and representative institutions is never completely divorced from those smaller interactions and expressions that make up everyday life, gestures that ultimately constitute and function as the social lifeblood of these formal frames and larger institutions. Thus, the dialogue that passes for much of public discourse, promoted under a banner of impartiality and in the best interest of all, is never so universal as to ever be completely disconnected from those more embodied, emotional, and personal concerns. And as these particularistic concerns—once formulated at some distance from the official public sphere—become more and more directly involved in public debate, affairs, and policies, they also increasingly become the very ground for resistance and social change (e.g., see Goldfarb 2001).

In this respect, at a time when much current debate revolves around what is and what is not political, atheist blogs, sites, and videos derive at least part of their significance in promoting the nontrivial nature and importance of secular concerns and issues in public discourse, expanding secular discussion, and creating news and forums for debate. In addition, as means for empowering atheists to represent themselves, these media create new forms of virtual association and activism around not only political issues concerned with inclusion and the separation of church and state—long a concern of secular organizations and atheists in particular—but also cultural issues concerned with identities, norms, and alternative values. Just as feminists and the LGBT community have focused on creating political identities from previously underrepresented concerns, atheists are bringing their expressions of nonbelief and atheist concerns into the public sphere as well.

Against this backdrop we can better understand the historical shift, noted by Bradly Nabors (2009) in his study of secularist organizations. The shift took place from a predominantly institutional secularist activism focused on legal proceedings, building coalitions with religious organizations, and fighting for church-state separation to a cultural secularist activism stressing the role of argument and debate and associating itself with science, actively trying to discredit religious belief outside the sphere of law, and advocating for change outside the channels created for this purpose by the dominant secularist organizations. Such a distinction follows the split found in the literature on social movements between political and cultural movements (Eder 1993). Understanding this distinction in secularist terms, the former seeks to maintain the secular nature of government and challenge forms of domination at the level of the state. The latter is primarily interested in cultural change and attempting to construct secularist and atheist alternatives at all levels of the existing social order. In this respect, the cultural approach is more radical in the sense that it is less inclined to see present social life as legitimate and less interested in maintaining the status quo, even within the secularist milieu and movement. Of course, in practice these two modes may not be mutually exclusive, and often secularist and atheist groups engage in both strategies simultaneously (a point to which we return below).

A challenge for understanding secularist activism includes the question of how to conceptually categorize such diverse subgroups in terms of a "collective identity" or "collective interest." Another issue is the relationship between secularist cyberactivism and secular organizations, on the one hand, and between secularist activism and politics (e.g., public-policy making), on the other. As one atheist author has noted,

[A]theism is *not* itself an ideology; there is no such thing as an "atheist mindset" or an "atheist movement." Atheism *per se* hasn't inspired and doesn't lead to anything in particular because it is an effect—not a cause—and there are countless reasons for a person to not believe in God, ranging from vicious to innocent to noble. The newborn baby lacks a belief in God, as does the Postmodern Nihilist, the Communist, and the Objectivist—but each for entirely different reasons having dramatically different implications. So lumping all of these together under the "atheist" label as if that were a meaningful connection is profoundly confused. Yet this is exactly what the New Atheists do and encourage: they talk about how there are so many atheists out there, and advocate their banding together into an atheist community to seek fellowship, foster cultural change, build a political voice, and so on (Perkins 2008).

Perkins is off base in stating that all the new atheist authors uniformly see the need for a social movement. Harris and Hitchens have both argued that there is no need for one. Perkins does, however, sound a cautionary note on why one needs to be careful and qualify the use of the term "social movement" when looking at secularists, especially online. Consider some of the responses we received when asking about self-identification in a 2011 survey: "I find it difficult to choose between secular humanist and atheist. The first defines how I relate to humanity, the second defines how I relate to the universe," stated a sixty-seven-year-old Jewish man from New York City. A thirty-year-old male from Toledo, Ohio, on the other hand, said, "I prefer to self-identify as an atheist, despite the explaining and debate that sometimes requires (which I welcome), but I also consider myself a humanist and a freethinker." A forty-two-year-old woman from Tulsa said, "I'm a Unitarian, and somewhat quiet about my atheism, even among my friends." Another female respondent from Oklahoma said, "I say that I have no belief in the supernatural. Lately there has existed a group of persons who share my beliefs; they call themselves

'Brights.'" Political affiliations also ran the gamut—from the standard categories of socialist, progressive, libertarian, and conservative to the more idiosyncratic: "Depends," said a man from Texas. "I tend towards Libertarianism. I'm conservative (the old, pre-Reagan meaning) with regards to government spending and growth." A sixty-nine-year-old New York City attorney of mixed British ancestry said he was a member of the Socialist Party USA: "I call myself a Libertarian Socialist. By American standards, I am a howling radical. By the standards of the civilized world, I am an ordinary left Social Democrat." A thirty-year-old female of Russian Jewish ancestry from New Jersey said that she considers herself a "Libertarian but votes Democrat nationally and Republican in state elections." Finally, a sixty-year-old women from California who currently lives in Colorado confirmed, "I am a registered Independent. That doesn't surprise you, does it?" These few examples confirm that the secularist landscape is highly pluralistic, made up of multiple groups and subgroups, consisting of individuals holding diverse ideas and philosophies as well as divergent definitions of secularity and their own individual secularist self-identity, even as they share some level of consciousness. As Hitchens, referring to secularists, has stated, "We're not a unified group. But we're of one mind on this: The only thing that counts is free inquiry, science, research, the testing of evidence, the uses of reason, irony, humor, and literature, things of this kind" (Hitchens, qtd. in Cipolla 2007).

Our focus on the pluralistic nature of secularist collective action online in this chapter should not distract one from the definite patterns of secularist identity and ideology (Kosmin and Keysar 2009; Pasquale 2010), and the recognized ways in which one becomes an atheist (Smith 2011). Yet too close attention to cohesion and a unified identity misses the tensions and divisions related to identity formations within the secular milieu (Cimino and Smith 2011; LeDrew 2012) that are intensified, at least partially, due precisely to the fact that the collective identity they are united by prizes independence and autonomy. Another factor has to do with the variety of collective histories and intellectual traditions that comprise atheist identities (e.g., see LeDrew 2013). Also, in many respects, this is a first-generation collective or group identity: an identity achieved (Smith 2011) rather than given—that is to say, inherited or passed down from one's parents, family, or tradition. Finally, religion is often understood in terms of being a community or a "religious movement" and is often conflated with a general group or herdlike mentality by some atheists—a point that helps explain some of the opposition to any notion of a secularist community or social movement among some secularists, even as they undoubtedly constitute one.

When the question "Would You Be an Atheist without the Internet?" was asked on the Friendly Atheist blog (2009), respondents tended to answer in the affirmative, with many saying they came of age and became an atheist prior to the advent of the Internet. Nonetheless, almost all those who commented stated that they would be less active, less informed, and less aware that they were not alone without such technology, a pro-Internet stance also confirmed in our questionnaire. That many respondents to our surveys and atheists online use the pronoun "we" and start sentences saying, "As atheists...," confirms the presence of self-awareness based around a group consciousness and a movement mentality. Such recognition that there are like-minded individuals beyond themselves goes hand in hand with the expansion of the communicative conditions of contemporary media—the very technologies that other communities and critics bemoan for producing an atomized lifestyle—to imagine and produce a "community of reason" (to use Pigliucci's term) from the ground up.

VIRTUAL SECULARISM VERSUS ORGANIZED SECULARISM?

One of the more noteworthy aspects of secular activism online is the fact that much of it is coming from the bottom up, from individual users not affiliated with any formal organization. Traditionally, secularists have had their protests and declarations represented and mediated through secular organizations, including their publications. Secularist organizations were the only channel for such explicit activism, offering a smooth transition between the "private" participant's cultural values and the institutions that represented these values to the "public." Insofar as secularists recognized themselves in the values of these organizations, there was no problem. Of course, it's easy to speak for the majority when the cultural means of symbol and message production is limited to a few, achieving the appearance of unification and consensus due to the limited number of participants in on the decisions and views expressed within such institutions.

Viewing the Internet as a form of social communication that simultaneously changes the nature of the experience secularists have among each other as well as the experience others have of secularity helps us understand the changing role of secularist organizations. In discussing the impact of digital media on skeptic organizations (which seek to debunk alleged paranormal and supernatural phenomena), Daniel Loxton (2009: 24) states,

> [The Internet] changes everything. It's true that digital outreach may bring new grassroots support to traditional skeptical organizations, but realizing that potential requires facing up to a more fundamental shift: traditional skeptical organizations are no longer the default leaders of the popular movement. Indeed, new skeptics may not even realize the traditional skeptical groups exist.

What is crucial is not that secularists online are advocating for change; secularist organizations have been doing this all along. Rather, the significant thing is that they are advocating for change outside the avenues created for this purpose by the dominant secularist organizations, even as they build and draw on the work of such organizations (even if unknowingly). These new forms of online advocacy and activism have the potential to simultaneously strengthen and undermine such organizations' legitimacy. They can strengthen such organizations by pursuing actions parallel to their activities and, more directly, by "contributing money, buying magazine subscriptions, [and] sharing Web links" (Loxton 2009: 27). Yet these new forms of activism can also undermine such organizations insofar as the demands, desires, and discontent of these "independents" cannot be adequately integrated into and articulated through such organizations. To the extent that this happens, and continues, such organizations have two choices: face a crisis of legitimacy or adapt and change to meet such demands. The latter option is arguably what the CFI opted for when Paul Kurtz was voted out as the organization's chairman, later resigning altogether in the face of critiques from those he labeled "angry atheists." Of course, as Massimo Pigliucci (2010b) noted in a blog post responding to an earlier version of this chapter, "We also have to remember that people like P.Z. [Myers] see CFI as accommodationist, and in their view not in sync with the grassroots." While this is true, it nevertheless confirms the undermining of the hierarchical organizational form and the weakening of social institutions, such as the mainstream media and press, as authoritative sources of information and knowledge. Such organizations and institutions, while still important, are no longer taken as the only legitimate avenues for airing grievances and articulating discontent.

Antonio Gramsci (1971: 5) once observed that "every social group, coming into existence … creates together with itself, organically, one or more strata of intellectuals." This is as true of atheists as it is of any other social group. Nonetheless, in contrast to the activist tradition that looked to intellectuals as a vanguard to lead the people, the relationship between atheist intellectuals and the everyday secularist is better conceived of as a dialogue as opposed to an imposition. Many secularists indeed look to intellectuals like Harris and Hitchens as leaders, given the advantageous position that they occupy within the secularist milieu and movement, one that is clearly mind heavy and intellectually oriented in posture and content. Intellectual leaders are obviously important in secularist activism, exercising a degree of social and cultural capital that lends them disproportionate influence.[5] And many lay atheists view and think of themselves as part of a vanguard.[6] Nevertheless, the nature of practice online—connecting each actor to multiple intersecting networks, which online secularist activity reflects and perpetuates—provides the individual secularist with a means to come out and speak out without institutional support in a way and on a scale that didn't exist previously, altering the balance and relations that exist between institutions, intellectuals, and unaffiliated individual actors.

Secularist activism online might be considered a soft activism. However impassioned and contentious the debates and flame wars, and regardless of the fact that many secularists have appropriated the term "militant" to refer to themselves, in the last analysis, much of the social antagonism is based on the expression of subjective opinions. However, having different ideas about the best way to proceed or tackle particular issues without having the ability to actually make collective decisions or reach a consensus online does not mean that secularists are uninterested or incapable of doing so offline. To the collective aspects of such activism we now turn.

VIRTUAL AND ACTUAL ACTIVISM AMONG SECULARISTS

Some research (such as Diani 2000) suggests that computer technologies are more effective at strengthening existing bonds than in fostering new ones. Our study suggests it cuts both ways: the Internet strengthens community "globally" and individuality locally, as well as generating consensus in terms of a loosely affiliated movement and broad culture. In other words, the expansion of communication technologies and networks allows atheists to be simultaneously more individualistic and more collective. In addition, some evidence suggests that the decentralized movement of secularity shares an effective affinity with the decentralized nature of the Web and digital communication technologies to a degree that other more centralized and hierarchically oriented movements do not. To the degree that this is the case, atheist activism and protest perhaps have a better chance of succeeding and reaching their objective insofar as they are congruent with the technological situation, especially when factoring in that secularists (statistically) tend to be on the more well-off side of the digital divide.[8]

We also believe that technology can forge new bonds, especially among the younger secularist demographic due to their heavy Internet use coupled with the growth of secularist organizations on college campuses across the country. Frank Pasquale's (2010: 79) observation that "secularism continues to replenish itself with younger participants" may well lie in the potential of such communicative networks as a medium for the formation of new secularist groups and their recruitment into existing organizations, especially since there is reported to be an overrepresentation of nonaffiliated young people among Internet users.

Regardless of whether any substantial growth has taken place in the number of secularists due to computer technologies, the cyberactivism of secularists has certainly had an impact in cultural and organizational terms. Secularist organizations that had once restricted their activity to more accepted and standard strategies have adopted the methods of protest initiated by those more radical and vocal individuals and groups, proving that attractive cultural productions, strategies, and messages do not always emanate from the center. Again, CFI is a good case in point, with Ronald Lindsey promoting projects that CFI founder Kurtz objected to, such as International Blasphemy Day and a contest soliciting cartoons attacking religion. However, the question of whether such activity has had the same success in political terms as far as policy making and agenda setting is a more complicated question, because they are essentially different sides of the same movement.

The secularist organizations existing prior to the Internet did not explicitly object to or position themselves against more grassroots or identity-oriented initiatives and associations. Painting the shift from instrumental to expressive, or from institutional to cultural, as a linear and all-or-nothing occurrence is thus inaccurate, since information and influence have flowed in both directions and on both sides: organizations have adopted the cyberactivists' postures and methods while "independents" have supported, joined, and built on the work and activism of various organizations (Smith and Cimino 2012).

The idea that the primary target of secularist activists has strongly shifted from the political and legal spheres to the cultural and academic spheres (Nabors 2009), insofar as their methods and strategies have moved in such a direction, is, at least to some extent, misleading. The stress on science and reason and discrediting religion has expanded and increased, but this has not displaced legal concerns, such as the struggle over the separation of church and state, a form of activism supported by secularists of all stripes. Secularist lobbying groups also target the political sphere directly, which many independents support through financial contributions. This two-pronged strategy suggests that when speaking of the prospects for secularist mobilization, such an opportunity should not be framed in terms of the movement as a whole. Various causes and situations may be better addressed by a particular strategy or segment of the broader movement—the new atheists, for example— and may influence and modify the rest of the relevant actors and organizations (Gamson and Meyer 1996; McAdam et al. 2001).

Contemporary secularism is a blend of organizational forms and independent actors and thinkers. The former seeks to position secularists as part of a broader American public, though they also simultaneously position themselves as minorities seeking to align themselves with other groups that are also left out of the mainstream, and detest the influence that religious groups and religion in general have politically in the United States. At the same time, these organizations—occupying a cultural center in the movement, constructing discourses aimed at the official public sphere, and functioning as the public face of the movement, with at least some comparative economic and political power—distance themselves from more aggressive atheists and more contentious issues that would put them at greater odds with the mainstream and make it harder to engage topics with broader appeal (such as civil rights, separation of church and state, and the ills of religious extremism) that many Americans share. Yet independents, speaking as a subculture from the margins, have the freedom to formulate particular and often more attractive messages aimed at the cultural base or grass roots. Further, they can promote and spread a more aggressive critique not only of religion, but also of the notion that public discourse must necessarily operate within the framework of acceptable civil discourse and the liberal ideal of neutrality with respect to religious beliefs (or lack thereof), without worrying about the need to make their views and advocacy more palatable to a broader public. These differences also highlight the fact that the way you seek to make your message more acceptable or palatable to an outsider is rarely, if ever, the way you take pride in your own identity among your peers.

All of this relates more to the relationship between secularist activism and secular institutions and does not really tell us what influence, if any, secularist cyberactivism has had on politics more generally. A good amount of commentary is available on the link between new information technologies and politics. To take one example, Jeffrey Goldfarb has looked at the role the Internet played in the Howard Dean (Goldfarb 2001) and Barack Obama (Goldfarb 2009) political campaigns, specifically with regard to grass-roots organizing and initiatives. Studies have also looked at the role that social media has played in other parts of the world, such as the Arab Spring.

Research has found that "seculars" (those not affiliated with a religion) are significantly less likely than church members to belong to other organizations, to volunteer, or to contribute to charity, thus lacking the social capital generated by the religiously affiliated. As of 2008, however, seculars were considerably more likely than "religious traditionalists" to make use of the Internet for information about the presidential campaign (Hansen 2011). And with such technology increasingly playing a greater role in politics (Davis 2009), there is the potential to move beyond past limitations, especially when we consider that activism online not only runs parallel to offline activity but can also incite it. This suggests, again, that instead of an opposition between the organizational and the grass roots, contemporary secularity is better thought of as existing along a continuum of various compositions, identities, and strategies, occupying and aimed at the center, at one end, and emanating and speaking from the margins, at the other. However, this center-margin schema is contextual: one identity or strategy may be privileged in one situation or place (e.g., online) and marginalized in another (e.g., the official public sphere). The key is to pull back and see how these diffuse constellations—which on the surface often appear at odds—are being networked together in broad coalition and work as, at one and the same time, a movement, a subculture, and a community *united in difference*.[9]

Offline atheist activism has grown significantly in the last decade—particularly new organizations and umbrella groups, such as the Secular Coalition of America—to coordinate action on church-state separation and discrimination against atheists. Moreover, the level of political activism and engagement among secularists continues to grow. In fact, secularists have engaged in coordinated, collective action in their approaches to legal cases, protests, rallies, and advertising campaigns. Secular alliances and strategies have shown a measure of success against efforts by the religious right to restrict abortion and gay marriage and introduce intelligent design into public schools. For instance, the Freedom from Religion Foundation, reporting a membership of fourteen thousand, scored a major victory for secularism in 2010 when it won a lawsuit that declared the National Day of Prayer to be a violation of the First Amendment (Hansen 2011).

Of course, atheists specifically have had the problem of not having a channel to influence political parties in any direct way; most American politicians cannot afford to align themselves explicitly with atheism because the consequences would be too severe. In fact, only two politicians to our knowledge to date—Rep. Kyrsten Sinema, Democrat from Arizona, and Pete Stark, the former

Democratic congressman from California—have come out as athe-ists. Secularists arguably have the numbers to exert substantial influence in the political arena. They have made great strides politi-cally, both online and off, and recent research shows that when it comes to social issues, secularists tend to be largely "progressive" (Williamson and Yancey 2013; Flynn 2012a) and politically aligned somewhat left of center; they generally favor government interven-tion on issues of education and limiting the influence of religion, while holding to more libertarian ideals and a live-and-let-live atti-tude in the private realm.[10] These stances could allow for joining existing coalitions on the Democratic left (functioning as a pres-sure group) while simultaneously working toward realignment and reform (breaking apart established positions within the two-party system) at the grass roots, but no well-worn, established path is cur-rently in place to do so.

Of course, political opportunities, resources, and the support of powerful allies are not the only issues a movement has to con-sider. In fact, without a mass constituency willing to support sec-ularist issues and causes, no institutional or structural change will suffice for success. A mass constituency, in fact, is a prerequisite for any type of social collective to emerge. This point precisely, in terms of developing a group consciousness based around broadly similar agendas and ideas and secularists' recognition of their commonality and their expression in collective action online and off, is where the positive attributes of secular cyberactivity and activism can be seen as having the most influence. Of course, the criticism is valid that a genuine community consists of more than individuals weakly connected via a computer screen and keyboard. Part of this something more is a sense of coordinating actions together in a particular locale, as opposed to spread out across different time zones. This sense of "coordinating actions together" is the cornerstone of sociality and social rituals. Such sociality can draw on a wide variety of forms and personnel configurations, in a wide variety of contexts and locales. These varied and mobile repertoires of interactive rites and rituals, and the experiences such actions produce within the atheist milieu, are our subject in the next chapter.

Chapter 4

Ritualizing and Commemorating the Secular

Sanderson Jones seemed caught up in the spirit, even if he would adamantly argue that it wasn't the Holy Spirit. With his shoulder-length hair and beard, Jones bore a resemblance to Jesus, or at least an Old Testament prophet, but he played the part of a Pentecostal preacher as he paced the platform, punctuating his exhortations with short leaps. "We're reclaiming the soul, transcendence, ecstasy—all feelings that are inside of us. We start at zero and end at zero. . . . Atheism is the diving board and life is the ocean. We're made up of atoms but we're having the best time that atoms can have in the universe. . . . It's an amazing gift not believing in God. You have to have an attitude of gratitude—be happy you're an atheist!"

This secular yet mystical homily that one of the authors witnessed on a summer Sunday afternoon at Tobacco Road, a "bikini bar" in midtown Manhattan, was part of the first leg of the American tour of the Sunday Assemblies, a movement of atheist "churches" that Jones and fellow stand-up comedian Pippa Evans had started in London in early 2013, drawing a crowd of up to six hundred. Already fifteen Sunday Assemblies were planned to be launched in the United States by September 2013. Although it is difficult to know when some atheists are being serious and not engaging in irreverent satire, Jones and company actually do model the assemblies after churches—at least churches that sing Beatles and Fleetwood Mac songs rather than hymns and venerate community more than God. Just like in a church, there were testimonies (about "coming out as an atheist"; it was gay pride Sunday in New York, so the theme of coming out was played up at the event), an offering, and even a moment of silence where participants could "talk with themselves" about how lucky they were to be atheists. Rites of passage, including funerals, weddings, and baby naming ceremonies, will also be held in these assemblies.

Jones may call himself an "atheist missionary," but he is not a very polemical one; he even seeks cooperation and advice from established churches. While he has faced some criticism from secularists for downplaying science and reason, Jones said that he cofounded the Sunday Assemblies to reach those atheists' "not being reached by other atheist groups.... Most atheists may value the intellectual and cerebral approach to things; the only problem is that most people don't." Only a few months later, the Sunday Assembly experienced its first schism. The New York City Atheists had taken part in the assembly from the beginning, but they gradually began to have misgivings about the soft-sell approach of the Assembly and Jones. Jones started discouraging the use of the term "atheist" and the gatherings seemed too churchlike to many atheists. Eventually the NYC atheists formed the Godless Revival as an alternative to the Sunday Assembly, which itself moved from meeting in a bar to the New York Society for Ethical Culture.

Jones's kinder and more spiritual face of atheism is partly a response to the new atheism (another British import) and its polemical stance toward religion. Its growth and divisions mirror the fractious landscape of American atheism and humanism.

Even though it is sometimes called the "new new atheism," this camp actually harkens back to older humanist ideas and practices. This conciliatory atheism reemerged in the heat of battle between the new atheists and theists, calling for a truce with religions as well as summoning secularists to develop a more positive identity (although many atheists would see their atheism as being more than just negating a belief in God).

Part of this agenda, as outlined in such books as *Good Without God* (2009a), by Harvard humanist chaplain Greg Epstein, and Chrisf Stedman's *Faitheist* (2012), is to cultivate a coherent ethical system, a greater sense of community, and the practice of rituals. In this chapter, we look at the prospects for a positive atheism (though not necessarily one identified with Epstein's project), both through a survey of participants in atheist and secular humanist groups as well as by an examination of something we call "secular spirituality." We also examine secular commemorations and rituals as specific examples in the broader effort of revitalization, through both ethnographic observations and textual analysis.

Although a large segment of secularists eschew the need for rituals, claiming that they have left such rudiments of religion behind, we argue that rituals play a particularly important role in organized humanist and atheist circles. We found that various kinds of secular rituals and other symbolic forms, such as commemorations, can play different functions; they may generate solidarity between atheists or play a legitimizing role for secularity in wider society. As we have noted in earlier chapters, the drive toward a conciliatory or positive secularism has a lengthy pedigree in the United States. There has long been a tension in organized atheist groups between debunking or attacking religion—whether in a defensive or offensive mode—and trying to build community and a positive secularist identity. Positive atheism was evident in what was called religious humanism in the mid-twentieth century, which was most strongly embraced by the American Humanist Association, Ethical Culture, and a significant segment of Unitarian-Universalists. The use of the word "religious" was meant to stress experiences and activities that are humanly significant, while excluding any supernatural beliefs and explanations of reality, but the term has served to divide the various camps of atheists.

In more recent years, a form of positive atheism can be seen in the secular humanist movement, which is defined as a system of ethics rather than a movement attempting to negate theism. Paul Kurtz, founder of the Council for Secular Humanism, stressed this point about the positive nature of secular humanism in contrast to the new atheism, although at first he was strongly supportive of these writings (a change in attitude that played a part in his resignation from the council). Kurtz (2008) also increasingly spoke of the need for rituals and an appeal to the emotional and aesthetic as well as the intellectual and scientific domains of life in establishing secular humanism.

In his book Epstein harkens back to religious humanism as he calls for secular versions of weddings, funerals, and baby naming ceremonies, and for observing secular holidays, such as "festivals of light" and solstices as substitutes for Christmas and Hanukkah. He also popularizes and reworks secular rituals and practices for secularists who are largely unaffiliated with atheist or humanist organizations. Using a functional definition of religion, Epstein proposes such alternatives as meditation (to induce the relaxation response); cognitive or rational emotive behavior therapy, which he calls the secularist equivalent of prayer; and cultivating a renewed appreciation of art.

ORGANIZED SECULARISTS AND THE "NEW NEW ATHEISM"

How has the "new new atheism" circulated and been received among secularist organizations? Inspired far more by Kurtz than Epstein, the Council for Secular Humanism has started a "secular celebrant" program to provide officiates for nonreligious weddings and other rites of passage. At the same time, as mentioned above, there has been controversy and divisions about the place of the new atheism in the council's leadership, with a general consensus favoring the new atheism and its more oppositional views and approach. In the council's magazine *Free Inquiry*, there is considerable resistance and opposition to the more conciliatory forms of atheism and humanism. In a review, Tom Flynn, editor of the magazine, portrays Epstein's book as unearthing the long-standing differences between religious and secular humanists. While praising the book as "the best short introduction of unbelief I've seen," he goes on to note how Epstein's spiritualizing tendency, as seen in his discussion of the importance of myths and his stress on the need for a secularist community, conflicts with secular humanism. Secular humanists have "lost faith in faith," ruling out any "assent beyond the evidence ... myth is always a dirty word," according to Flynn. Likewise, he adds that "many secular humanists fail to see the value of congregational life. For them to 'fall back on the ritual ... to fall back on something' [as Epstein writes] is instead a challenge to muster the courage to resist that siren song" (Flynn 2012b). The magazine has shown little sympathy for atheists seeking any accommodation with religion. In an editorial critical of the phenomenon of young atheists appropriating some forms of religion for their own use—such as fasting during Lent—and taking a less oppositional stance toward believers, Flynn writes that such secularists are playing with fire by ignoring religion's powerful and dangerous influences. Just because many young atheists did not grow up under oppressive religions, Flynn warns them not to be "too quick to decide that this wolf has no teeth" (Flynn 2013).

In this chapter we are specifically interested in what people active in secularist groups think about the proposition that atheists should focus less on debunking religion and more on building a positive identity. What are their views on the importance of and their participation in secular rituals in their groups? Finally, we are interested in what they think about "secular spirituality"—the idea that various activities and practices create feelings of awe, wonder, and even transcendence, while eschewing any belief in supernatural reality.

We asked 167 participants in secular humanist, humanist, and atheist groups about these issues in an Internet survey. Although it was not a random sample, we attempted to obtain fair representation of the various organized secularist groups throughout the country. However, we especially focused on the secular humanists represented by the Council for Secular Humanism, not only because they are the largest subgroup of secularists, but also because the umbrella group, at least under the leadership of Paul Kurtz, has been advocating some of the above changes. Our results show that most of the respondents clearly want to retain the role of debunking religion, even if the "new new atheists" might discourage it. While they may still want to develop a positive image and agenda for secularists, most don't want to discard their skeptical and even polemical edge toward religion. At the same time, almost half of respondents agreed that ritual needs to be given more attention in their organizations; only 26 percent disagreed with that statement. But only 35 percent had attended a secular ritual (we did not count those who cited rituals outside of these organizations, such as family events, Burning Man, and sporting events), but almost 62 percent said they would be open to participating in such ceremonies in their groups. There were some strong dissenters. As a seventy-nine-year-old self-identified secular humanist stating she was turned off by our survey put it, "The word 'ritual' drips with religiosity. Conformity is inherent in the meaning of the word. Atheists are 'free thinkers' and as such are quite capable of creating and personalizing celebrations uniquely appropriate to each of their life events." She went on to assert that she would feel uncomfortable participating in a secular group that performed rituals and "would question the focus of such a group as being not truly atheistic."

Yet over 32 percent said rituals of some kind should have a regular part in their meetings. Most of these rituals involved rites of passage, such as weddings, funerals, and baby naming ceremonies. But there were more unusual ones, including de-baptism, where atheists would renounce their baptism, usually with the help of a hair dryer, and winter solstice celebrations. There was some ambivalence about the role and effects of rituals. Only 29 percent said they felt a sense of community through participating in rituals; just as often they said that they found such a sense of community themselves in the secularist meetings—based largely on intellectual discussion. As for the emotional effects of awe, wonder, and a sense of belonging to something greater than themselves, only 12.5 percent reported feeling such emotions in these rituals.

We wanted to know if the participants ever felt these transcendent feelings, or what we call "secular spirituality," in other activities as well. First, we found an interesting subgroup of 23 percent who refused to answer this question on secular spirituality, with some commenting that no such thing exists for an atheist. A significant percentage of those who did answer seemed to confirm some of Kurtz's and Epstein's observations and proposals for a more positive secularist movement embracing aesthetic and emotional dimensions as well as science and reason. While being in nature (59.2 percent) and working in or reading about science (47.9 percent) rated the highest, these activities were closely followed by performing or listening to music (47.3 percent), admiring or doing art (41.9 percent), and meditation/contemplation (35.3 percent). There may well be a wide divide between those refusing to answer this question and those viewing mediation and art as providing a secular spirituality. There may also be differences between those who see science as a source of such emotions and those viewing the arts as such as the locus of a secular spirituality.

More demographic analysis is necessary to understand this dynamic, but the younger respondents—a population that has traditionally had a low representation in organized secularism but represent the growing edge of the movement—were more likely to select art and meditation in this question. It may be the case that these newer groups are coming into the ranks of organized secularism and arriving at an atheist position in general through aesthetics and the humanities—even a kind of spiritual seeking we described in chapter 1—rather than through the traditional paths of science and philosophical rationalism. While secular humanists and atheists have sharply criticized postmodernism for downplaying the role of reason in society, it could be that potential atheists influenced by postmodernism in the humanities may have found an alternative route to secularism and atheism. It may also be the case that the greater availability and abundance of media have opened up a wider path (beyond sociobiology, science, rationality, etc.) for secularist socialization, exploration, and participation. The appeal of the Sunday Assemblies and their secular-spiritual approach among many young adults may also be a sign of a generational shift among secularists over these concerns.

Our findings on secular spirituality are reflected in emerging research. Scholars have mined a secular spirituality in everything from popular culture and "fandom" to the high arts and aesthetics (Carroll 2011). In a study of theists and atheists in the United States and Germany, Heinz Streib and Constantin Klein (2012) found a small subset of atheists and nontheists who identify as "spiritual but not religious." Such atheists are open to "horizontal" rather than "vertical" transcendence, meaning that they found spiritual meaning in nonsupernatural worldly and earthly activity. Streib and Klein concluded that these more spiritual nontheists, particularly in the United States, are also characterized by higher openness to experience as compared to either religious or strictly secular groups. Frank Pasquale (2010) found that 38 percent of the secular affiliates he surveyed use the concept of spirituality in a psychological and experiential sense. Interestingly, Pasquale found a surprisingly high percentage of secularist group participants (30 percent) who were willing to believe or consider the notion of an impersonal force "coursing through and connecting all living things." He also found that those most likely to describe themselves as "atheistic" or "antireligious" were most averse to "spirituality." We found something similar, with many respondents confirming the positive role of ritual in their life while adamantly disavowing any notion of spirituality therein. As a sixty-five-year-old, ex–Roman Catholic respondent stated, "I have certainly felt awed or elated when observing nature, listening to music, admiring art, and on other occasions. I don't consider it to have a spiritual component. 'Secular spirituality' sounds like a term coined by those who say 'I'm not religious, but (please don't burn me at the stake!) I am spiritual.'"

VARIETIES OF SECULAR RITUALS

The rituals and practices we have observed so far in person and on the Internet (through YouTube, for instance) have used meditation and contemplation and, in some cases, art as well as personal sharing in their events and meetings. This is not something particularly new for a religious humanist group such as Ethical Culture. The Ethical Culture service that one of the authors attended included a "colloquium" that opened with taped music by Beethoven and an observed silence for about five or ten minutes as people sat around a circle. The leader of the group then introduced the topic of pride, asking each participant what he or she was proud of in their lives. Each one shared events or achievements that gave them a source of pride. After that the music came on again, this time Mozart, and another five minutes of silence was held. Some of the participants closed their eyes while others stared off into space. After the leader recounted a story about pride, participants were free to express their further thoughts about the topic before the meeting closed.

A more formal service followed that was based on a talk given by the director of the society on the value of music. But again there were moments of quiet and contemplation interspersed between discussion and announcements. After the service I found that the event drew a diverse following. Included were secular and religious humanists as well as one woman who said that she espoused a belief in God, noting that at first the old-time members had difficulty with such a belief but had grown more tolerant over time. But all agreed that formally religious elements, such as prayer, should have no part in the colloquy and the service.

One might expect these quasi-religious practices at a "religious humanist" group such as Ethical Culture, but the event was very similar to a secular humanist gathering in New Jersey. The leader was introducing meditation practices to the group, again mixed with personal sharing. Phillip, the leader of the group, opened the meeting by rubbing a small mallet against a Tibetan prayer bowl, producing a piercing ring that reverberated through the small meeting room. The bell signaled for the six participants sitting on metal chairs and a couch that it was time for meditation. As silence filled the room for the next five minutes, it was easy to wonder if we had stepped into the wrong meeting. "It's not the usual kind of secular humanist meeting," Phillip admitted. The CFI website initially described the group as promoting a "secular spirituality," but it was feared that people would get the wrong idea and the word "spirituality" was quickly deleted. But Phillip's description of the group sounded spiritual:

> This is very visceral, not only intellectual. Humanists are very cerebral. We're trying to get what you find in a church but in a secular manner. We need to be in touch with our feelings, more aware of mind-body connections. We talk about a secular journey that's equivalent to spirituality. It's the sense that we're all connected. Science can inform us that separateness is an illusion. When we tune into that connectedness and a sense of awe and mystery about ourselves ... that's precisely what spirituality is, shorn of all that [religious] baggage.

After the brief meditation session, Phillip called for those present to make a small circle with their chairs. The session was part encounter group and part science lesson. A biofeedback device was passed around as participants were asked to share negative experiences in their past. Reggie, a man in his mid-forties who worked as a sleep researcher, recounted the tense and frustrating relationship he experienced with his doctoral supervisor in graduate school. This professor tended to forget and ignore Reggie's proposals for his dissertation, at one point even forgetting his name. He was never able to finish his dissertation due to the professor's inattention and indifference. As he described the hit-and-miss encounters with his absent-minded professor, the biofeedback device started whirring louder. Reggie was clearly relieved to hand over the device to the next group member. After most participants shared bad experiences, they were encouraged to engage in role-playing to better understand their problems, as well as to understand the situations of the people causing them distress.

We wondered how the participants related this activity to their secular humanism. How was this different from any other form of group therapy? As if to answer my question, Phillip concluded that "humanists' dealings with other human beings are difficult, especially with irrational people. People in organized religion have pat answers to make them feel better. We can't give pat answers." Laura, a cheerful woman in her forties, remarked, "Religions are good as a Band-Aid. . . . They tend to draw in troubled people, where we look to the best of psychology and science."

With the rites-of-passage ceremonies, we see a different dynamic in play. These rituals are not only intended to unite a group of people; they also seek to be "effective" in a more specific way. For instance, wedding ceremonies seek to be effective in celebrating the union of two individuals for families and friends, while funeral services are largely seen as a providing a source of consolation for the bereaved. Many of the texts used for these rituals in secularist groups are authored by Jane Wilson, a British humanist, although the secular celebrants we interviewed also write their own and draw on texts common to a group such as CFI.

The funeral ceremonies suggested in these texts follow what can be called a low-church Protestant style, which is not unusual considering the influence of Unitarian-Universalism in organized secularist history. The service is structured around opening words, followed by thoughts on life and death, a tribute to the deceased, a simple committal of the remains (usually cremation), and then closing thoughts. These texts obviously show a strong this-worldly quality; funeral ceremony texts, for instance, stress the importance of the deceased having had a full and fulfilling life. The particular personal qualities of the deceased take precedence over a general service for the dead. Mourners are asked to look beyond their grief and to celebrate the relationships and contributions of the deceased that will remain. The references to nontheism are clearly stated in most such funeral texts. As one humanist funeral text plainly states, "Those of us who accept the unity of the natural order, and believe that to die means the end of the conscious personality, look death in the face with honesty, with dignity and with calm." Memory is thus the central component of the secularist funeral, with mourners being asked to remember the deceased during happy times of their lives. Throughout the ritual there is a de-emphasis on intense emotion, with the celebrant balancing mourning with celebration of the deceased's life. The role of literature and poetry should also be noted. All of the samples we studied recommend that celebrants read or play recorded poetry and prose throughout the ceremony, believing that such recitation "can soothe and release pent-up feelings in some people which will help in the long process of grieving" (Wilson 1990).

In a similar way, the wedding ceremonies outlined in the texts are also low-church in structure and style. More improvisation tends to take place in wedding ceremony texts, with the secular celebrant program at CFI offering a variety of sample ceremonies that can be used for particular occasions (such as committal and same-sex ceremonies). But the ceremonies tend to be structured along the lines of, first, opening thoughts about marriage or partnership, and then reading from literature and particularly poetry on the subject. The vows are then exchanged, with the prompting of the celebrant. The main ritual, besides the exchange of rings, is the lighting of a "unity candle," which symbolizes the sharing of "energy and love" between the couple. The couple is asked to express their love and equal responsibility to each other while they exchange rings. Perhaps somewhat unusual for an atheist ceremony, a CFI sample ceremony text includes a closing American Indian blessing (although without reference to a deity) just before the couple is pronounced married or partnered by the celebrant.

Many aspects of the secularist culture gain potency by standing somewhat apart from the larger society. Yet, insofar as innovations often are easier to institute and find less resistance on the margins, this "standing apart" is a position of opportunity for secularists. The idiosyncratic nature of the services and ceremonies we observed, which are as acts of bricolage that decouple practices from a traditional context and reinvent them anew without any anxiety regarding authenticity or linking such practices to traditions in the past, speak to such opportunity.

SECULAR GATHERINGS AND SOLIDARITY

Aside from explicit rituals, it could be argued that secularist gatherings and events function as rituals as well in that they serve to symbolize unity and strength to both themselves and the outside world. This could be seen at the 2012 Reason Rally in Washington, DC, that we described in chapter 1.

The large video screens positioned around the National Mall where the event took place allowed participants to view themselves as part of a significant gathering. The rally not only served to physically mobilize secularists in a particular location; it was also an event that acted to emotionally liberate and strengthen solidarity among participants in highlighting their common identity, allowing participants to come out and speak out as secularists. The speeches, music, and especially the comedy, not to mention the confrontations with Christian protesters, managed to meld these independent freethinkers into something of a convivial community. These secularists, who within their particular meetings and groups often engage in open and critical debate among and about themselves and their own diverse identities and interests, publicly came together and took their respective and collective interests and identities for granted. In this way, they put on a unified public front and performance. Despite different opinions, agendas, identities, and interests, then, these freethinkers found a common rallying point, *not within but against.*

Almost every secular humanist and atheist meeting we attended began with a session devoted to poking fun at the foibles of religious groups and people, or with a performance of music satirizing religious themes. In her study of British secular humanists, Susan Budd (1977: 266) found that the condemnation of religion in these groups can "act as a protective ideology, since it becomes a defining characteristic of the movement and a method of uniting otherwise dissident opinions." As a symbolic affirmation of values, secularist rallies often use humor to render pressing concerns and future desires into a communal experience. Strategically using humor helps constitute public rallies as festive, carnival-like spaces separate from the mundane, where secularists can suspend ordinary roles and reality. Within this context, participants are invited to express themselves and collectively mock their adversaries in ways not typically afforded them in their everyday lives. In this way, rallies act as a mechanism not only for in-group integration but also for creating a ritualized space in which challenges to the status quo and symbolic hierarchies can be carried out. Other avenues for secularists' self-legitimation and redefining their position and identity in American society involve commemorations.

As organized secularity has expanded the interest in and debate about the importance of rituals, commemorations, celebrations, and other observances have become more common. This interest has manifested itself throughout history with numerous attempts to create new holidays, rituals, and other rites of passage to mark secular events and movements. This can be seen in the attempt of the French Revolution's architects to wipe the historical slate clean, abolishing holy days and observances, including the Christian calendar's trajectory originating in Christ's birth. In its place, the inauguration of the revolution was established as Year One, accompanied by a panoply of observances of revolutionary "saints" and commemorations to legitimize and celebrate the new order. Organized secularism, at least in the United States, was modeled on a low-church Protestantism that generally eschewed observances, not to mention developing a cult of saints and martyrs. Yet as contemporary secularism has sought to provide a community for atheists and compete with theists, there have been several attempts to create secular holidays and commemorations.

Two of the most prominent of these observances have been the winter (and, to a lesser degree, summer) solstice and Darwin Day. Since the solstice celebrations are also shared with neopagans and New Age practitioners, it is difficult to study many of these events as strictly secularist observances; many atheist and humanist groups list general solstice celebrations that are not strictly secular in makeup. The winter solstice celebrations sponsored by secularist groups are often treated more like holiday celebrations (usually held at a restaurant), for those uncomfortable with Christmas, but show minimal atheist or humanist content. HumanLight is another secular alternative to Christmas, celebrating the "humanist values" of tolerance, compassion, empathy, honesty, free inquiry, reason, and rationality. The event was started in New Jersey by the New Jersey Humanist Network in 2001 but does not appear to have spread throughout the secularist community. In a similar way, Blasphemy Day, which was established both to celebrate freedom of speech and to attack religious values, was started by more hard-line atheists and has not been taken up by the softer humanist groups. For this reason, we focus on Darwin Day as the most prominent secularist commemoration.

DARWIN DAY 2012 AND SECULARIST LEGITIMATION

Darwin Day did not naturally evolve as a commemoration on the secularist calendar. The first Darwin Day was organized by the humanist community at Stanford University in 1995, although there were earlier Darwin celebrations. Massimo Pigliucci, a secular humanist philosopher, also independently initiated an annual Darwin Day at the University of Tennessee in 1997. These commemorations were intended both as an homage to Darwin and as a celebration of science for the secularist and academic community. A national organization to coordinate Darwin Days began in 2000. The event became more widespread in colleges and universities around the country, which also served to create an important link between academia and secularist organizations. Commemorations can be defined as events that unify and provide identity to the people or groups celebrating them, but from our observations of four Darwin Day events in the New York–New Jersey area in 2012, we found that these observances play a part in legitimizing secularism to a broader public.[1]

"Screw the creationists! We don't care about them. Science has already answered them. This is the day to celebrate science," said Calvin Dane, the director of Long Island's Ethical Humanist Society, when one of the authors asked him why the society's Darwin Day event did not pay much attention to creationism. It was the society's fourth Darwin Day commemoration, and like the others, a scientist was invited to lecture on an aspect of evolution. A gathering of about seventy-five to one hundred members and visitors filled the society hall as the service commenced with a rap song about Darwin's discovery of evolution. Signs and handouts with "Darwin fishes" lined the auditorium. The lecture was a fairly scholarly account of natural selection. The lecturer made no reference to atheism, and only during the question-and-answer session did someone ask about creationism and its claim that the creation of the eyeball was proof of an intelligent designer. After the lecture, a leader told the congregation that the commemoration was "not about debate but about inclusion. Here everyone can come together over science." After a guitar-and-vocal rendition of the theme song from the sitcom *The Big Bang Theory*, everyone was invited to a science fair, as the society's children had set up exhibits and experiments throughout the auditorium. The irenic and innocuous tone of the event seemed planned. In an interview Dane said that Darwin Day is a way that the Ethical Humanist Society reaches out to the community and especially to children. The event always draws visitors, and some attendees have become regulars and joined the society.

Even in the more strongly atheistic secular humanist society in New Jersey where we observed another Darwin Day, the tone was more formal than polemical. Aside from selling Darwin and evolution fishes, the event, attended by eighty to one hundred people, was based around a scholarly lecture by a biologist on the myths and misconceptions of evolution. Interestingly, Darwin was introduced as a "deeply spiritual but not religious" thinker, and there was little criticism of organized religion or Christianity.

A Darwin Day event held a few days after the event in New Jersey at a secular humanist group on Long Island, which might have unsettled Charles Darwin himself, showcased more of these diverse views. The scientist who was scheduled to speak could not make the engagement, and after a brief talk by a member, the meeting morphed into a freewheeling discussion on evolution and its implications. A man with a southern accent said that evolution raises more questions than answers and that the "theory is running into dead ends." Another attendee asked, with some puzzlement, "What is this fascination with Darwin among secular humanists? Darwin had a big part in [explaining] the structure of the universe and our place in it. We do depend on experts. We have a right to ask how he did it." One of the members shot back in an exasperated tone, "We need a holiday to promote and celebrate science and rational thinking—it's an important way to get together and affirm that." A middle-aged woman turned the discussion to the controversy of teaching evolution and questioned the need to interpret the theory in a nontheistic light: "Why can't we just teach evolution and let people attach their faith to it if they want?" Strangely enough, we later found out that some of those questioning the secularist interpretation of evolution were regulars of the society; the small group had two ministers who attended the events, often playing devil's advocates, while others defined themselves as agnostics (we learned that the secular humanist group had lost its charismatic leader and other members over the years).

Strangely enough, only at a Darwin Day event at Hofstra University on Long Island did the strong critique against creationism and even theism that one might expect to hear from secularist organizations receive a prominent place in the proceedings. The university had sponsored Darwin Day events for a decade, often in a celebratory manner, including a huge cake, dramatic presentations, and one of the professors dressing up like Darwin (with obligatory muttonchop sideburns). These events have included a joint Valentine's and Darwin Day conference on Darwin and Sex, and a reenacted debate between Darwin and David Hume and how they would address intelligent design.

The Darwin Day celebrations at Hofstra began when one of the professors was trying to find a way to teach evolution after visiting the Museum of Natural History with students. During this time, another professor heard about the national organization and decided to link up with it to publicize their event. There was no association with the secularist groups that had first inaugurated Darwin Day; only after holding the event at Hofstra did the organizers learn that secularists were also commemorating the day. But the 2012 Darwin Day at Hofstra clearly had creationism in its line of fire. The first presentation by a geology professor showed footage from the creationist video *Darwin's Dilemma* and argued that the fossils record used by creationists disproved creationism. Other presentations criticized intelligent design and religion in general as being unscientific. These are fairly standard views found in most science departments at universities. But we were struck by the fact that the secularist organizations' celebration of Darwin Day that we observed tended to stress the positive elements of science rather than the negative nature of religion, while the university event had a more explicitly antireligious theme.

An examination of the Darwin Day listings for 2012 by the national organization suggested a strong academic orientation. The commemorations were either sponsored by a university or by a group such as the Student Secular Alliance, or were special programs of a secularist group featuring a recognized scientist or scholar. The academic pedigree of these commemorations helps enhance Charles Darwin's role as a "secularist saint" among atheists and humanists. The question of whether Darwin was an atheist and whether evolution endorses atheism is part of the broader political and symbolic struggles in the United States around the relationship between science and atheism. Atheists like Richard Dawkins and PZ Myers actively promote the view that there is a positive correlation between science and atheism, wherein knowledge and study of the former inevitably leads one to the latter. A more moderate position is expressed by those like Eugenie Scott and Stephen Jay Gould, who argue that religion and science necessarily ask and address different questions and aspects of the human condition, and are therefore not necessarily incompatible. Flanking the extreme end of the antiscience, postmodern spectrum is sociologist Steve Fuller, who assertively seeks to disavow any link whatsoever (be it historical, social, or cognitive) between science and atheism and propagates the idea that intelligent design is scientifically legitimate (which he argued at the 2005 Dover school board trials, no less). Finally, there are those atheists like Jerry Fodor who challenge and critique certain aspects of Darwin's theory of evolution.

Coalescing with the growing academic interest in naturalism, the influence of neo-Darwinism and the "turn to nature" evident in disciplines from psychology to economics creates a growing place for organized secularism in academia and among scientific elites. However, Darwin's recognition by the wider academic culture and American society more generally is of most use for secularists in their quest for spreading the good news of science and creating a more positive, populist identity.

SECULARIST RITUALS AND THE CULTURE
OF FREETHINKING

Secularists understand ritual differently than their religious counterparts. What we take away from rituals varies according to what we bring to them. Secularists bring an overriding concern with remaining independent and freethinking, and one of their main "collective" activities/activism remains debunking religion and theism. This helps us make sense of a few things. First, it explains secularists' aversion to the term "spirituality" (and the reason some respondents disliked or disapproved of the term "secular spirituality"). As noted, throughout our survey, we had respondents both confirm the positive role of ritual in their life and deny any spiritual component to such. It also allows us to understand why secularists view personalized and less formal rituals more positively. As a sixty-year-old secular humanist from Pittsburgh, Pennsylvania, put it, drawing on the herding cat analogy (an analogy that was mentioned more than once by different respondents), "In this cat herd, each will decide his own preference." Often respondents were reluctant to be too specific regarding the whole issue, stating that it is up to each individual to decide for themselves what they need, want, and find pleasure in, and if they want to participate in rituals.

"What makes religion distinctive from everything else," argues Randall Collins, "is announced in its symbols, which affirm the existence of a sacred realm explicitly higher than mundane life" (2010: 4). Where religion has historically understood ritual as a means for becoming part of a larger community and transcending "the worldly," secularists understand ritual as a means for celebrating oneself as human and dwelling in a contingent world. For secularists, rituals are less about group integration and more about creative meaning-making grounded in an emphasis on the individual. Any community-oriented rituals seem to be largely of secondary importance for secularists. In fact, when we asked about the community-generating nature of rituals, the respondents (when not outright dismissing the need for community) often stressed that their local meetings fulfilled their need for community.

Even the most individualistic of religions still places a sacred figure or text at the center of its rituals, whereas if we wanted to draw a comparison among secularists we could, at best, maybe point to an intellectual personality or a "canon" of texts (perhaps the writings of new atheists) similar to what one might find in an academic discipline. The comparison to academia is apt given the intellectual and mind-heavy orientation of the culture and the fact that science is the main meaning structure that secularists draw upon to "replace" religion (Smith 2011), even as science is detrimental to meaning-making insofar as it has been the one of the main sources of disenchantment (in the name of truth and the search thereof) in the modern world. This disenchanting and demystifying aspect of science is one of its main draws for secularists and their fostering of an oppositional culture in a society that is viewed as religious, irrational, and anti-intellectual. Moreover, in terms of activism, secularists are not using science to pursue the truth per se; they are using the authority or cultural power of science to press their claims. In this respect, the issue of whether atheism can rightly claim a prominent place in the progress of scientific achievement historically, or whether atheists presently have a correct view or understanding of Darwin's legacy, is inconsequential. More consequential, in terms of politics, is whether such a scientific discourse and narrative can be a strong resource for a more mainstream, popular mobilization in the United States. Using the rational authority of science is different than using the moral authority of God. Religious interests can connect their political motives and goals to God's will. They can also mobilize their constituents more easily due to the inbuilt community ties and a stronger organizational infrastructure (where there are often strong links between individuals rooted in local settings and larger organizations and institutions at the state and national level). Science, at least as a practice, remains open to contestation and revision by its very nature in a way that religion does not. For this reason, using science as a stable cultural resource and an ideological tool for political ends, organizing, and community-building is more difficult than using religion, an issue that secularists, insofar as they have goals beyond the epistemic, will have to continue to address. No doubt knowledge of this matter is in the background of Epstein's and Kurtz's call for a more positive atheism, an atheism perhaps informed by science but rooted in a humanistic, universalist ethics.

Downplaying the focus on science can also be found in Alain de Botton's controversial call for secularists to use religion. De Botton—who claims that the most boring question you can ask about religion is whether the whole thing is true—is concerned with how to adapt or reorient certain aspects of religious ritual tradition without replicating what he sees as problematic in religion, going so far as to suggest an atheists' temple for nonbelievers to meditate. When asked in an interview why atheists throw away the useful aspects of religion, de Botton had the following to say:

I think it's because of a great intellectual honesty: I cannot scientifically appreciate God so I'm going to have to leave all that behind. I'm going to have to give up all those benefits because something doesn't make sense. That's a very honest and very brave, lonely decision.... All sorts of things have become impossible because they seem too religious. There are any number of moments in secular life when atheists say "oh, that's getting a bit religious isn't it." I think we need to relax about approaching some of these areas—they don't belong to religion, religion happened to sit on them. They're for everybody. (Lawton 2012)

Sam Harris—a hard-liner, and one of the so-called four horseman of the new atheism—has come out in defense of the positive aspects and usefulness of meditation as well, stating that one can practice it "without believing anything preposterous about the world." And, like de Botton, he has expressed some frustration with the fact that "many atheists reject such experiences out of hand, as either impossible, or if possible, not worth wanting" simply because of the religious association (Snider 2005; Harris 2007). In expressing such views, de Botton and Harris have faced critiques from fellow nonbelievers. PZ Myers (2012), in one of the harsher responses, referred to de Botton as a "fence-sitting parasite" who, in advocating the use of religion, sees "a personal opportunity to pander to the believers" for his own personal gain. *Free Inquiry* editor Tom Flynn (2005) accused Harris of allowing his ideas to become muddled on account of his use of spiritual language. Flynn's and Myers's adherence to a hard-nosed, hard-won rationalism commits them to oppose sociological (read "sympathetic") views of religion and ritual that would rationalize such by pointing out the positive function they serve for the individuals involved. To point out that there is some deep-seated human need for ritual, or that engaging in such action satisfies psychological needs for participants, is little more than religious apologetics for Myers (2011b) and Flynn (2012b). As Myers (2011a) assertively argued in a post on Epstein's use of religion as a model to structure atheist meetings, "No gods, no masters, no dogma, and no goddamned priests. . . . not even atheist priests."

It is hardly surprising to find that the term "spirituality" or the idea that nonbelievers should use religion give many atheists pause for concern and incite condemnation. It's going to be a hard sell to convince the majority of atheists that "mysticism is a rational enterprise" (Harris 2004: 221). Spirituality and mysticism carry a negative connotation and are synonymous with religion for many nonbelievers. In his lecture "The Problem with Atheism," the same lecture in which he defends spirituality, Harris makes the case for not self-identifying as atheist on account of the negative perceptions attached to it. Such advice significantly downplays the strong, and often primary, identity commitment atheism holds for many secularists. To self-identify as atheist—sometimes at great emotional and social cost—is a meaningful achievement for many, not a default position of indifference, nor simply a condition of the absence of belief in a society that is already sufficiently secularized. Nonbelievers don't have a problem self-identifying as atheists; they have a problem with the fact that self-identifying as such is a problem at all. In fact, it is precisely this strong, personal identity commitment—often archived against traditions and belief systems they were socialized into within a cultural environment where religious belief still tends to be the norm—that leads American secularists to rhetorically valorize reason above all else and defensively rebel against anything that even remotely reeks of the religious, including rituals.

Yet, on a second look, these public performances and self-secularity rituals clearly show that secularists are interested in more than reason or science. Science in some form or another may inform and play a huge role in secularist practice and culture. This does not, however, mean that individual secularists are not interested in activities and practices beyond science. As our research has shown, secularists are involved in a host of experiential and expressive activities—from appreciating music and art to contemplating and experiencing the marvels of nature, from meditating and practicing yoga to expressing one's self through the arts. Such activities don't necessarily compete with their understandings of science and their secularist practice but can actually complement them. For example, at services and weddings, music is used to set the mood or meditate on the wonders of nature; at rallies, humor is employed in talks, lectures, and mockery; and many respondents pointed to the importance of the arts in their life and activism. Of course, why should this not be the case? Secularists are human, after all. The fact that this has to be pointed out speaks to the fact that secularists often suffer from the same one-dimensional stereotypes they are so often accused of perpetuating against religion. Moreover, in looking at the recent literature, it is hard not to come to the conclusion that atheists have spent a far greater deal of time thinking and writing about religion than religious people ever have of atheists as a group. Atheists are always imagining what the world looks like from a believer's point of view. Of course, nonbelievers have had no choice but to try to understand religion; that believers now occasionally are forced to consider the other side speaks to some form of success.

RITUALS AND THE SECULARIST FUTURE

Many approaches to ritual do not consider the capacity or power of ritual to possibly transform and act back on the reality from which it was borne, yet the rituals we have observed point to this potential. The rites-of-passage celebrations, such as wedding ceremonies, show how secularists can borrow and reinvent ritual symbols and styles from one context and redeploy them in another. Insofar as these ceremonies are not merely construed as "civil" but "secularist" or "atheistic," they stand out as an alternative juxtaposed between the power of the church and the indifference of the state in presiding over such occasions.

If the self-secularity rites of passage constitute a form of latent protest, secular social gatherings and rallies constitute a manifest form. Public gatherings, such as rallies, mobilize secularists in a public, ritualized space where they are invited to heighten and intensify their atheist identity and momentarily suspend other roles, identities, and concerns. Forms of humor and mockery are one of the important expressive dimensions that help form these freethinkers—who engage in debate among and about themselves and their own diverse identities and interests—into a unified collective temporarily, even if they may intensify stigma from the outside. Simplifying complex concerns and desires, humor is important not only for attracting broad participation but also for enabling rapid diffusion of the atheist message. Another important component of this diffusion—which further highlights the important role of humor and mockery within the secularist milieu—is related to the expansion of communication technologies and sites such as YouTube, which both atheist personalities and the lay secularists use. Finally, Darwin Day events—which are coupled with an assortment of other events like the weeklong Darwin Festival and Evolution Sunday—are platforms to celebrate and inform the general public about evolution and Darwin's life specifically, and to promote scientific literacy more generally. Such events are seen as especially important in the United States due to the high percentage of people who do not accept the evidence for the theory of evolution. Hard-liners argue that a positive correlation exists between understanding and studying science and someone becoming an atheist. In this view, Darwin Day events—as one of the strongest points of convergence between atheism and academia—may stand as both a commemoration rite and a first step on the road to deconversion. More research is needed regarding the effects of these commemorations and rituals. Regardless, the less such a relationship between atheism and evolution is made visible, the better it is for generating a positive public reception and securing such an event's socially meaningful status on the annual calendar.

So where does this leave things regarding the fostering of a positive secular identity? Certainly, many in our sample agreed with Kurtz and Epstein on the importance of rituals. However, a significant number did not. Insofar as atheism remains an oppositional identity in a culture of normative theism, this is to be expected and is unlikely to change anytime soon. In assuming a secularist identity, many atheists have had to reject the traditions and rituals they inherited through birth or those that were imposed upon them. There is also the inherent tension in championing modern science and trying to construct some positive, psychologically satisfying narrative from a worldview that is designed to satisfy rational requirements first and foremost, and is largely indifferent to those meaningful referents (including fictions, myths, and illusions) that impose "a recognizable, meaningful order upon the continual shifts in sentience to which we are inherently subject, so that we may not only feel but know what to feel and act accordingly" (Geertz 1973: 80). All this, no doubt, makes secularists self-conscious, reflexive, and quite conflicted on the merits of rituals, and helps explain why secularists in the United States have sought alternative understandings and styles of ritual related to issues of identity, community, and a repudiation of religious belief within the secularist milieu. What remains to be seen is how this oppositional identity may manifest itself in the second or third generation of secularists, when perhaps the transfer of information about atheism and secular humanism will be less contentious and conscious and merely a matter of socialization and tradition.

Conclusion

During a Friday night meeting of secular humanists on Long Island, slides were being shown of a secularist gathering, one of which showed Christian protestors bedecked with signboards demanding that atheists "Repent and Believe." Amid the guffaws and jeers, one of the members in the front piped up, "Ya gotta love em!," which just elicited more laughter. This remark, whether said in jest or not, reflects some of the symbiosis that we have observed between secularists and religious believers throughout our research.

As discussed in chapter 1, we often found a measure of enjoyment, even camaraderie, mixed with exasperation in the confrontations between atheists and religious believers. A recent survey confirms that secularists are quite knowledgeable about religion, even more so than many believers, and it is difficult to believe that accruing such knowledge is just a matter of knowing one's "enemy." Even if materialistic and consumer society may be indifferent to philosophical and religious concerns, secularist and religious antagonists are interested in and actually delight in engaging larger questions of meaning. The fact that secularists and believers need each other can be seen in the frequent debates between evangelicals and prominent atheists, as well as in the political sparring that takes place between defenders of strict church-state separation and supporters of religious accommodation (where mutual hostility is the most intense, probably because the stakes are so high).

We have attempted to show how atheists and the secular humanists define themselves by their rejection of religious and societal norms, and how their creation of alternative systems of ethics, community, rituals, and even "spirituality" is often shaped and influenced by American religion. For their part, religious believers define atheists as the "other"—the personification of unbelief from which they seek to differentiate themselves in creating a moral community—actions that can and often do have political implications.

That secularism exists as a social movement in relation to religion is most evident in the United States, where religious institutions, belief, and involvement retain significant vitality. But even in seemingly secular societies, atheist and humanist movements have been formed and revived through corresponding religious upsurges and incursions. In secular strongholds such as the Netherlands, Denmark, and Britain (the exporter of the new atheism), the growth and new public role of Islam has reignited atheist activism and politics. The largest humanist movement in Europe is in Norway, where it grew in proportion and reaction to the power of the Lutheran state church. As we hinted at in our first chapter, the present and possible future of organized atheism and humanism in the United States hinges on the prospects of institutional and, to a certain extent, noninstitutional religion. In other words, revisiting the question about the connection between secularism and secularization will tell us a good deal about the future of the "atheist awakening."

DISENTANGLING SECULARISM AND SECULARIZATION

Whether and to what degree America is undergoing secularization are widely debated. The term itself has several meanings, but for the purpose of this Conclusion, we stress its most common usage as the inevitable decline of religious beliefs, practices, and affiliation. It is helpful to see this process as being expressed on three levels— societal, institutional, and personal. On the societal level, on first impression, religion seems to be losing its influence in politics, the media, the arts, science, and education; the historic separation of church and state has encouraged this differentiation of the religious sphere from other areas of life (unlike in Europe, where church and state were conflated to a stronger degree than they ever were in the United States). But even here the signs of secularization are not clear. Even if there is no prayer in schools, our currency is still stamped with "In God We Trust," and it is still perilous for a politician to admit to atheism. Whether the various life spheres are in fact secular is also debatable. Popular culture—from graphic novels to rock music—is drenched with religious and spiritual imagery and references, while the fields of businesses, education, medicine, and social work have integrated spirituality—even if of the most generic sort—into their training and activities.

The institutional level concerns the vitality of religious organizations, and here we see a general pattern of stability and decline rather than widespread growth. But there is considerable variability as to which institutions are in decline; research has found that conservative groups and movements show greater growth and stability than liberal ones, but again we are faced with ambiguity and complexity. More lax nondenominational megachurches tend to grow more than strict fundamentalist Baptist congregations, and liberal and humanistic Unitarian-Universalists shows greater membership gains than many traditional churches. There is also the upsurge of the nonaffiliated (or nones), which relates to the final level of secularization consisting of individual beliefs and practices. Surveys regularly show a high rate of belief in God that has not changed significantly, even with a noticeable growth of atheism and agnosticism among young adults. But what is most noticeable are the steadily dropping rate of institutional belonging and a tendency to separate spirituality and religion. Whether the changes on this ground level will destabilize the upper levels of institution and society, leading to a stronger rate of secularization, is an open question. Revivals of personal religiosity have been known to "bubble up" and reshape the institutional and societal dimensions.

Social scientists have posited a number of factors that may trigger secularization—from increasing economic and existential well-being (Norris and Inglehart 2004) to religious pluralism and privatization (Bruce 2002) to the advancement of science and technology (Wilson 1982). We have seen that it is Wilson's hard-line secularization thesis that secularists throughout much of their history—from Auguste Comte to Richard Dawkins—have most closely embraced: the advancement of reason and science will naturally shrink the role of religion in the modern world. But as we have discussed, scholars and secularists themselves have questioned that thesis. The general slope of secularization is supposed to point down to indifference about religion—not the furious engagement with religious claims displayed by the new atheism. Even pluralism has not led to the widespread privatization and irrelevance of religion as predicted by secularization theorists; as noted above, the public reemergence of religion—either by way of religious terrorism or Muslim immigration—generated a more public atheism at the turn of the millennium even in very secular nations (Bullivant 2012). Peter Berger (2013) writes that aggressive atheism is more an expression of pluralism than secularization, since the "co-existence in the same society of competing beliefs and values undermines the taken-for-granted status of all of them, religious or secular." Today the indicators in the United States and around the world point just as clearly to long-range conflict between secular and religious parties as a loss of religious vitality (Fox 2014). As Michael Ian Borer (2010: 137) concludes, "When we see the new atheists as an 'embattled' minority, intensely fighting against the religiously devout and faithful, we can see just how much people have held on to their religions as the primary source of meaning and order."

The above thumbnail sketch of secularization and religious vitality in present-day America suggests that the advancement of organized secularism may face some success along with several obstacles. Sustaining the atheist awakening will largely depend on the fate of the nones: will they remain in a no-man's land between secularism and religious affiliation, or, as they move through the life cycle and raise their own children, will they gravitate to one side or the other? Recent research suggests that millennials' disaffiliation from religion "may now be hardening into a rejection of religion per se, and not merely of organized religion," according to the political scientist Robert Putnam. He notes that between 2005 and 2011 the national Faith Matters surveys found that "among 18- to 29-year-olds, the 'nones' rose from 25 percent to 33 percent, while the number of atheists and agnostics (those who say they do not believe in God or are not sure about God's existence) rose from 15 percent to 24 percent. Among older cohorts the comparable shift toward atheism/agnosticism was from about 9 percent to about 12 percent" (Cimino 2012).

Another study finds that more recent birth cohorts that were raised with no religion hold more secular beliefs. This may be because marriage may no longer encourage a switch to a religious preference as in the past, since the growing number of unaffiliated young adults provides a pool for marriage partners of similar backgrounds. Members of the younger cohort also show differences from older ones in their higher rates of political liberalism and lack of confidence in religious organizations. Because political liberalism and lack of trust in organized religion are associated with decreased odds of a switch to religion, the younger cohort may be the carrier of a long-ranging secular trend (Merino 2012). Other studies, however, show that the niche for atheism in American society has remained small for a long period of time—4 percent of Americans disavowed a belief in God in polls both in 1944 and 2007 (Stark 2012). Of course, there is evidence that Americans tend to exaggerate their religiosity when polled (Hadaway et al. 1993), whereas one finds the opposite in Western Europe—a fact that highlights the significant role of normative religiosity in the United States.

Yet even if nonreligion grows as an individual preference, this does not necessarily translate into organizational gains for atheism or secular humanism. The high degree of individualism and independence among secularists makes for many nonjoiners. The fact that most of the growth in atheism has come from young adults who, as an age group, tend not to be joiners may make recruitment all the more challenging; showing up at the occasional mass rally or local meeting may demonstrate interest in atheism and spur some to activism, but it does not lead to stability and growth of a social movement. Rallies and movements intersect, but they are not one and the same. At the same time, we have tried to highlight the strength of these weak ties among atheists, specifically online, based around a set of core ideas and experiences that are leading to growing solidarity among the irreligious on the ground.

Even though there is a new (or actually revived) level of confidence among secularists that they are on the winning side of history and progress—at least compared to the early 2000s when we began our research—it is fragile and not shared by all atheist and humanist leaders and participants. As late as the summer of 2013 Tom Flynn, the editor of *Free Inquiry*, counseled caution to his secular humanist readers in taking an overly rosy view of secularism's future in the United States. He argues that religious influence abounds in American society—from renewed gains in the prolife movement to media fixation on the election of Pope Francis—and that secularists still must rigorously engage the "battlefield of ideas" against the "illusions" of religion (Flynn 2013: 4).

Of course, if the battle for secularism was ever "won" in the United States, where would that leave atheist activists and organizations? In one sense, it is in the interest of organized secularism to promote optimism and confidence among its participants to keep the momentum of the movement going, something we see with some leaders too eager to conflate the swelling numbers of nones with actual or potential secularists. But declaring victory too soon throws into question the need for atheist activism and solidarity and can easily lead to complacency, especially in a society where religious upstarts and vitality sprout up rapidly and in unexpected places. This is a dilemma that many underrepresented and marginal groups and identities experience, for they are caught between emphasizing the notion that they are on the winning side of history and the culture wars, on the one hand, and the opposite notion that they are minorities and outsiders and losing the battle in some respects, on the other. Both strategies and rhetorical approaches, as we've tried to show throughout this book, coexist and can be used to propel atheists to action and further mobilization. The tension between the need for more progress and the fulfillment of such progress keeps the movement going. Perceived and actual discrimination persists, yet secularity is increasing in many aspects of social life. Religion is, at the very least, no longer the default position or naively considered natural, but is rather one option among others in many parts of the country.

Detecting the growth of secular culture, let alone secularization, often depends on one's vantage point. The country remains religiously divided along regional lines, and the same geographic divisions can affect the fortunes of organized secularism in different ways. In a strongly religious region, such as parts of the American South, cultural secularity is obviously weaker. Religion is still taken for granted in such areas. The question is not whether you are religious but what religion you are. Atheists and secularist groups essentially function as a subculture in such regions of the country, holding ideas or beliefs that are distinctive enough to make them identifiably different from the surrounding culture. Nonetheless, such groups show great vitality—in direct proportion to the great need—already revealing a growing young membership (when compared to the Northeast, for example). Additionally, such groups have the potential to serve as a counterculture, generating a "cultural challenge that precedes or accompanies political mobilization" (Poletta 1999: 1). In strongly secular regions, on the other hand, organized secularism may not necessarily be weaker (having access to secularized and cosmopolitan elites in such fields as academia, publishing, the media, and politics), but it often takes on different expressions—for instance, moving from serving as a source of support for a minority population to focusing on outreach and education to a surrounding area and population that are already strongly secularized (Christina 2013).

At the national level, the question of whether a direct correlation exists between highly religious areas and secular growth in the form of "disbelief" organizations or "organizations that promote secularism" remains open. Recent research finds "evidence that disbelief organizations emerge as a response to the local prevalence of conservative Christians" (Garcia and Blankholm 2013), and other research holds that membership rates in such organizations tend to be lower in states where non-Christians have filed high numbers of lawsuits to protect their religious freedoms, and also in counties that vote Republican and have higher proportions of religious conservatives among all denominational adherents (Perl and Cimino 2011). That such organizations exist all over the country speaks to gains as well as to the work left to be done; their different forms and varied membership rates in different regions would be expected, given the different demographics and cultures. Secularism is a national reality that is also perceived differently according to one's social location and ideology. The conservative Christian watches the entertainment and news media as a swamp of unbelief and even antireligion, whereas the atheist turns on the television or flips (or more likely clicks) through the newspaper and is distressed by the way religion is still catered to in reporting, commentary, and advertising, while nonreligion is ignored or judged too hot to handle for the average consumer. The believer may see academia as dominated both by professors in the natural sciences who are materialists who deny the existence of God and those in the humanities and social sciences who espouse relativistic postmodernism and political correctness. The atheist may well applaud the upper hand that naturalism has gained in the sciences yet also bemoan the eclipse of reason in the softer disciplines under postmodernism and the tolerance for spirituality in university life as a whole, even as the demise of grand narratives conveyed under the auspices of postmodernism has helped call into question the certainty and truth claims that believers accord their religion. The secularist sees the wall of separation as too porous, while the conservative believer holds that it is too strong. Of course, America does not only consist of the religious right and the secularist left; in the large middle ground, secularism intermingles with religious belief without great controversy. But both the conservative believer and the secularist are right in sensing that what remains of mainstream culture and an educational establishment today still has to cater (or broadcast) to a largely religiously illiterate and tolerant populace—especially those under fifty—that nevertheless retains a memory and respect for religion and spirituality, even if in a generic form. For these reasons, strict believers are more apt to homeschool their children or send them to private schools in order to "narrowcast" and ensure that their beliefs are passed on and secular ideas and influences are minimized. In the same way, concentrated and controversial forms of secularism reach recipients through increased narrowcasting in the new and social media (with approaches toward broader audiences through cable TV comedy and bestsellers), allowing secular humanists and atheists to see themselves in terms of a wider community while providing new opportunities for activism.

FROM PROTEST TO POLITICS AND SEPARATION TO EQUALITY

The growth of atheist and humanist activity and organizations in the last two decades has obviously had a tonic effect on secularist identity. We see a secularist politics emerging, with a substantial majority of secularists being pro-choice, for gay marriage, and leaning left on social issues, with secularist identity and affiliation explicitly informing individuals' stances on these political issues, such as when a scientific understanding of sexuality leads to someone arguing for gay rights (Niose 2012: 87). Today there seems to be a stronger contingent of leftist organizations and media that are hostile to religion in general (or at least receptive to the new atheism), not only to religious conservatism—examples of this can be found in the atheist-friendly leftist news service *Alternet* and even the mainstream liberal magazine *The New Republic*. All of this reflects the trend of the Democratic Party increasingly serving as the home of secular voters. While libertarians—especially the Objectivist followers of Ayn Rand—have always had a large atheist constituency, the momentum, particularly in organized secularist discourse and activism, is toward political liberalism.

With increased publicity and notoriety comes increased opposition. As civil rights struggles have shown, one of the ways that social identities become politically salient is in opposition to discrimination, highlighting a discrepancy between the promise and the practice of the democratic process in respect to the (unequal) distribution of goods and rights. In the wake of the civil rights movement, many new groups—from feminists to gays to religious fundamentalists—have taken up the discourse of identity to struggle for equity and recognition in the political arena. As our book has shown, atheists are following suit. They are doing so by demanding representation and cultural recognition. Although such activism takes different organizational and expressive forms—from the everyday and mundane to the formal and organized—the goal remains the same: inclusion and autonomy. This distinction between inclusion and autonomy has run throughout the book, from the disputes between those who favor accommodation versus those who prefer confrontation to the different expressive forms found in organizational activism versus the more ad hoc and decentralized orientations found among independents. A recent example aiming at inclusion, discussed in the first chapter, is the name change from the National Atheist Party to the Secular Party of America in the hope to gain wider appeal beyond nontheists and collaborate with allies and ultimately give a greater political voice to U.S. secularists.

At the same time, secularist groups have sought and fought for cultural self-determination and equality in the same form that other minority groups have—going so far as to use equal-protection arguments in the court of law—while they continue to seek acceptance and promote their cause in the court of public opinion. Some activists even seek to legitimize their atheism through government accommodation in the demand for atheist monuments to be placed alongside religious monuments and for atheist chaplains to be added to the military chaplaincy.

SUSTAINING SECULARIST COMMUNITIES IN A FRAGMENTED CULTURE

The herding-cats analogy that we heard so often in secularist gatherings and interactions on- and offline confirms the difficulty that secularists have in fostering secularist unity and community. Numerous divisions among secularists are in plain sight—between accommodationists and hard-liners; between atheists content to focus on antitheism and humanists who stress secular ethics, social action, and rites of passage along with secularism; and between secularist men and women—not to mention the stubborn conflicts over politics and strategy that mark any social movement. A large number of secularists view their atheist identity in a way that is analogous in some respects to the identity politics embraced by racial and sexual minorities, whereas others resist such government accommodation, seeing it as diluting the oppositional and critical nature of atheism and giving their opponents ammunition to argue that humanism and atheism are religions like any other and therefore subject to "no establishment" restrictions—without all the perks that organized religion has received historically (Torpy 2013).

Some of these divisions are a rehashing of century-old conflicts in the freethinker tradition. For instance, the sharp differences we see over the need for rituals and a "secular spirituality" in secularist groups—brought to center stage with the publicity generated by atheists such as Julian Baggini and pastor-turned-atheist Jerry Dewitt promoting secular churches and performing secular services—replays the conflicts and controversies that emerged between religious and secular humanists in the mid-twentieth century. The debate over how much, if any, religion should be accommodated was probably voiced the first time atheists gathered together to form a society. Even Richard Dawkins, the doyen of the new atheism, has recently expressed his fondness for "mild Anglicanism," with its choral traditions and church bells ringing in every village square. Even if for strictly cultural-aesthetic reasons, Dawkins also criticized the penchant that American atheists have for seeking to remove crosses and other Christian symbols from public spaces (Murray 2013).

The important younger generations may not see this issue as worth fighting over; in the future, fewer are likely to be raised in strict or "oppressive" religious environments that would nurture a reactionary stance against all religion. Our Internet survey also clearly shows some division between generations in taking on an aesthetic approach to secularism—encapsulating its message in art and music, as well as through an emphasis on reason. This could be a result of the postmodern influence in American higher education, which has eclipsed the older forms of Enlightenment rationalism. But we have seen that both hard-line new atheists and softer and more accommodationist humanism have utilized the aesthetic approach; it is evident enough in the irreverent humor and music of hard-line atheist comedians and artists and in the use of symbols to protest and identify each other. Some symbols, such as the spaghetti monster and Darwin fish, being ironic appropriations of and juxtaposed to classic religious symbols of belonging, are used to challenge and mock, establishing what atheists and secularists do not believe or who they are not. At the same time, these symbols, which could also include Dawkins's scarlet "A" and the American

Atheists' atom, seek to promote the positive attributes of secularity while providing shared reference points and identity markers for members of a community with similar views.

These generational differences may highlight broader conflicts between scientific and humanistic atheists. The rise of the new atheism reflected and energized that segment of secularists who upheld the importance of science and reason in the atheist identity (Cragun 2012). Equally devoted atheists have stressed the philosophical, political, and artistic dimensions of nonreligion. We may see this simmering conflict come to a boil over the debate in secularist circles about transhumanism, a movement that presses for the lengthening and eventual transcendence of humanity through artificial and technological means. Although the movement has religious offshoots, the main architects of transhumanism are atheists who see transcending the human condition as the next stage of evolution. Religion scholar Abou Farman argues that, perhaps, "secular humanism and religion will find each other closer than ever before as the informatics cosmologists [his term for transhumanists] try and move away from both gods and humans, as well as from the earth itself" (Cimino 2011: 3).

Without venturing too far onto the shaky grounds of prediction, questions can be asked about the future viability of organized secularism in general. Historically and into the present day, scholars have noted the instability of secularist movements and groups. Attempts to collect numbers on the organized secularist movement as a whole usually hit obstacles, both because of the rapid growth of new secular groups and the disbanding of such efforts. Some of this difficulty results from the main growth of these groups in recent years being on campuses that are subject to the flux of student enrollment and interests. But humanist groups, particularly religious humanists that have membership bases with firm leadership structures, may show more long-term stability than the do-it-yourself atheist groups that have developed in recent years.

The nature of organized secularism may also change in the future. In our research in the New York area, we encountered two local groups—of secular humanists and religious humanists—that have moved (in one case somewhat unintentionally) to a format that resembles more of an open forum, including religious believers in debates and discussions, rather than as a center of atheist activism and mutual support. Whether this is an emerging trend, the structure of many secularist groups is open-ended and much more committed to free speech and a lack of dogma and traditions than a typical religious congregation, suggesting that they can accommodate a subdued secularist identity as much as an aggressive one. Organizations with strong identities, particularly in an antagonistic environment, are better able to compete and mobilize participants, so things can move in the other direction as well. The movement from a nominal or partial secular identity (where there was little consensus as to God's existence) to a much more outspoken atheist one can be seen in the evolution of the nationwide skeptical movement in the last two decades. In any event, if the trajectory of past forms of secularism and religious movements are any guide, the significant degree of ferment and conflicts we see in the first generation of the atheist awakening are likely to be replicated if not multiplied among the next generations. Ultimately, the success in handing down the fortunes of organized secularism to future generations will determine the movement's durability. The move to secular parenting education programs, secular camping, and other forms of youth engagement shows that secularist organizations are making a concerted effort in this direction.

SHARED COMMUNITIES OF MEANING

Should we leave the matter of the symbiosis and commonalities that we found among secularists and believers to the joys that both parties feel in the heat of battle and the mimicking of each other's strategies? Without having to sugarcoat the real and fundamental differences between atheists and religious believers, we think it is possible to conclude on a positive, if cautionary, note. As secularists are likely to gain a more equal footing with believers in the coming years, both groups may have to learn to deal with each other in new ways. Even if atheists don't grow rapidly in numbers, their increasingly outspoken and confident stance in society may make such engagement a necessity for the credibility of religious communities.

The popularity of the new atheist literature appears to have already convinced a segment of believers that they have to engage atheists in an intellectual manner where respect and civility rather than knee-jerk condemnations are among the ground rules. Catholicism, mainline Protestantism, and Judaism have the resources and traditions that provide a measure of social space to engage nonbelievers in common questions of meaning without having to "score points for the team." Pope Benedict XVI and Pope Francis have both spoken on the importance of dialogue with nonbelievers—a tradition that goes back to the Second Vatican Council (Speciale 2013). From the other side, the various humanist groups with a history of accommodating religion in one form or another lack the visceral opposition to all things religious that can make dialogue more difficult. Since evangelical Protestants are the main antagonists of atheists, with each party mirroring the tactics of the other, such nonpolemical conversations may be harder to sustain. But even the debates that have become the standard fare between evangelicals and atheists in recent years have unintentionally forged unlikely friendships where stereotypes and prejudices can be challenged.

Philosopher Charles Taylor (2002: 57) writes that because belief, unbelief, and agnosticism remain viable options three centuries after the Enlightenment, most modern people exist on the "cusp" between these two possibilities and may even "feel both pulls." According to Taylor:

> They have to go one way, but they never fully shake off the call of the other. So the faith of believers is fragilized, not just by the fact that other people, equally intelligent, often equally good and dedicated, disagree with them, but also by the fact that they can still see themselves reflected in the other perspective, that is, as drawn by a too-indulgent view of things. For what believer doesn't have the sense that her view of God is too simple, too anthropocentric, too indulgent? … On the other side, the call to faith is still there as an understood temptation. Even if we think that it no longer applies to us, we see it as drawing others. Otherwise, the ethics of belief would be incomprehensible.

The dark nights of the soul that ancient and modern believers experience may lend them an understanding of the mentality of atheists and agnostics, even as the "secular spirituality" claimed by many unbelievers may provide an inkling into the social psychology of theists (Novak 2008).

The most fervent and militant segments of the secularist and religious camps may well feel threatened by such encounters, for they always have the prospects of conversion and proselytization hanging over them. But the religious congregations and the emerging forms of secular activism and gathering that we have chronicled and studied in this book both function as communities of meaning—something both sides can recognize and engage beyond raging culture wars and politicization. They share a concern, even a passion, for ethics, values, and the common good that are becoming precious commodities in a consumerist and individualistic world. But for the near future, dialogue and empathy may have limited traction in a young social movement. They are more often the enemies of contestation and the oppositional milieu that sparked the atheist awakening in the first place.

APPENDIX

METHODS

Because this research was carried out over a span of eleven years, often based on a particular method in a specific time period for articles and presentations, we have grouped our discussion of methods according to the book's chapters. We have also included two online surveys that were distributed to participants in secularist organizations for our research included in chapters 2 and 4.

CHAPTER 1

Ethnographic interviews, participant observations, and textual analysis of secularist publications were the primary methods used in this chapter. We conducted forty interviews, mainly between 2002 and 2006. The remaining interviews were conducted during the Reason Rally in 2012. Fifteen interviews were conducted in the New York metropolitan area, and twelve in Tulsa, Oklahoma. These interviews were each approximately an hour in length. The remaining interviews were briefer and were conducted at the Godless Americans March in November 2002 and at the Reason Rally in 2012, both of which took place in Washington, DC.

The interviewees were recruited by attending secular humanist and atheist meetings and making public and private requests for participants and referrals for our study. The interviews in New York were recorded by hand, while those in Oklahoma were tape recorded. The interviews included questions on secularists' life histories, including whether they had religious backgrounds and training, the events leading to their espousal of atheism and secular humanism, and their involvement in organized secular activities. Additional questions focused on participants' views of their status as atheists and secular humanists in American society.

Participant observation was carried out from 2002 to 2012 in the New York metropolitan area, Oklahoma, and Washington, DC, at eleven meetings and rallies, sponsored separately or jointly by the Center for Inquiry, American Atheists, African-American Humanists, and the American Humanist Association.

Textual analysis of the Council for Secular Humanism's magazine *Free Inquiry* covered the period from the publication's founding in 1980 to 2011. Every issue of the magazine was examined according to the criteria stated above for the interviews.

CHAPTER 2

Media in the form of books, magazines, websites, blogs, and online forums play an important role in the social phenomenon of the new atheism. In highlighting the role of media in chapter 2, we focused on both the content and the medium. An analysis of articles devoted to new atheism in two magazines, coupled with responses by a sample of self-identified atheists on new atheism, allowed us to see how secularists themselves are interpreting and evaluating the new atheism. The medium is understood here as "a type of setting or environment that has relatively fixed characteristics that influence communication in a particular manner—regardless of the choice of content elements and regardless of the particular manipulation of production variables" (Meyrowitz 2000: 432). Examining both the content and medium surrounding how the new atheism is received allowed us to examine questions concerning how the media are reshaping relationships among atheists themselves, as well as altering the symbolic boundaries between atheists and theists.

Content analysis and medium theory both offer insightful approaches for studying atheism. Far from being incompatible, these two approaches can actually strengthen each other. Rather than setting the content as messages to one side and the medium as a context to the other, we believe that a more productive approach is "to have the assumptions, methodologies, and the object of analysis of each approach work itself, so to speak, into the analysis of the other" (Carpignano 1999: 178).

In focusing on how the new atheist phenomenon has been received and appropriated by those involved in atheist and secular humanist organizations, we first analyzed and discussed articles on the new atheism that have appeared in two of the most prominent secularist publications, *Free Inquiry* and the *American Atheist*, between January 2006 and March 2008. Second, we analyzed and discussed responses to a questionnaire (containing both open- and closed-ended questions) we created on the phenomenon of the new atheism (see page 170), as well as ethnographic interviews we conducted among thirty-seven atheists and secular humanists from an earlier study (Cimino and Smith 2007). The fifteen respondents for the questionnaire were found by way of a volunteer sample drawn from the websites and LISTSERVs of organized secularist groups. The only criterion for selecting such respondents was that they self-identify as atheist. Readers should note that we use "involved" here as a very loose category to capture those ranging from lone activists who engage in atheist protests to those who are active members of atheist and secular humanist societies to more marginal participants who subscribe to secularist publications.

CHAPTER 3

For the section on the traditional media in this chapter, we conducted textual analysis of the *New York Times'* coverage of atheism specifically in three decades, the 1920s, the 1960s, and the 2000s, although articles in other decades also were included for examination. For the section on the *Washington Post*, 150 articles covering atheism were analyzed in the newspaper from 1989 to 2013. The coverage before and after the emergence of the new atheism, around 2006, was given special attention. In 2008 we conducted an Internet survey in an attempt to gauge how atheists themselves viewed the role of the new atheism. We later adapted this survey (found on page 170) to develop the questions on atheism and the Internet. The questionnaire was distributed initially through the Secular Student Alliance (SSA) and its affiliates using Survey Monkey and Wufoo. Additionally, the survey was passed along through approximately twenty atheist and humanist groups with which we had personal contact. In the case of the local groups, the leader would post or send out the questionnaire, asking respondents to respond to us directly at our e-mail addresses. As one would expect, the local meetings garnered fewer responses from a smaller demographic, whereas the surveys disseminated through SSA and all its affiliates at the time (today it has 395) garnered many more responses from a much broader demographic, not based in any particular geographic region, bringing the total responses to 150.

To understand how atheists produce and distribute their own alternative media and culture, secularist websites, blogs, and YouTube videos were studied. Our selection of these sites was complicated due to the decentralized nature of the medium and the secularist community online. The sheer number and diversity of sites means that giving an objective account of secularist culture online is difficult. (For example, entering the term "atheism" in the Google search engine gives you 28.4 million results.) Sites were found by performing a search on Google using various terms, such as "atheism," "atheist," "new atheism," and "secular humanism." A further number of sites were identified by following links, quotes, and references—the equivalent of snowball sampling online—found on secularist sites, such as the website of the Richard Dawkins Foundation (richarddawkins.net). All together, we examined fifteen sites thoroughly and many more in passing, specifically focusing on prominent sites that get a lot of traffic, such as Reddit and r/atheism, as well PZ Myers's blog and Thunderfoot's YouTube videos, since they are still among the more popular secularist hubs online. We also analyzed other viral events we felt were relevant, such as redditgate. The blogs, videos, and sites identified and referenced all may be found via an Internet search, unless they are now inactive. All text from these blogs, social media sites, and websites were collected between September 2010 and August 2013.

These blogs and video accounts (or vlogs) are not only stand-alone sources for science and secularist information, they are also nodes within an increasingly connected secularist network. To this end, we tried to remain alert to the ways secularists understand and represent themselves online, while focusing on how the material conditions of mediation shape such an understanding and representation. Examining these sites and the content therein in this way—as part of a greater electronic culture—allows us to better understand the complexities of contemporary cyber-secularist culture.

CHAPTER 4

This chapter is based mainly on an Internet survey and participant observations of secularist rituals and commemorations. We asked 167 participants in secular humanist, religious humanist, and atheist groups about their attitudes and practice of rituals and "secular spirituality" in the survey (found on page 171). Although it was not a random sample, we attempted to obtain fair representation of the various organized secularist groups throughout the country. However, we especially focused on the secular humanists represented by the Council for Secular Humanism, not only because they are the largest subgroup of secularists, but also because the umbrella group, at least under the leadership of Paul Kurtz, has been advocating some of the above changes. Most of our responses came from the Southeast and Northeast, which have markedly different constituencies—the former being far younger than found in most other segments of organized secularism. Frank Pasquale (2010) found that the Pacific Northwest has the largest percentage of secular affiliates, so our largely eastern sample may not be representative of organized secularism in the United States. But generally, the demographic makeup of our survey reflects those of other studies, especially the greater proportion of men to women and whites to minorities who tend to participate in these groups (Pasquale 2010; Hunsberger and Altemeyer 2006).

Our participant observations of secularist rituals and commemorations included three meetings of an Ethical Culture society (a Darwin Day celebration and two regular services) on Long Island, New York; Darwin Day commemorations held at secular humanist groups in New Jersey (observed by Ayako Sairenji) and Long Island; and a Darwin Day event at Hofstra University, Hempstead, New York, in 2012. We also observed the first New York meeting of the Sunday Assembly in June 2012. We additionally used for this chapter observations and notes collected from the 2012 Reason Rally and other meetings we have attended over the last decade. We conducted twelve interviews (in addition to the ones cited in chapter 1) specifically on secularist rituals with members and leaders of these groups during our participant observations. These interviews were approximately fifteen minutes to a half-hour in length.

CONCLUSION

In one of the earlier studies of secularists in America, rhetorician Roderick P. Hart (1978: 36) expressed the relationship between religion and atheism thusly:

> Atheism and religion depend upon each other for significance. Without the one, exhortations about the other make relatively little sense. Apparently aware of this and of the fact that they have been declared failures as a pressure group, atheistic persuaders curiously turn to their old enemy—the churches—for both *raison d'etre* and psychological momentum. And as the grip of defeat tightens upon them, irreligionists increasingly depend upon their more successful partner for *rhetorical* initiative as well; they allow the churches to determine what topics are worth discussing as well as how and when those topics should be discussed.

To the extent that nontheists rely on the same (inverted) belief system as religion for their identity, is there any way for nontheists to not always be advocating an "antiposition"—a position in opposition to religion? Nietzsche (1967: 160) once quipped that atheism is not the absolute antithesis of the Christian ascetic ideal but "rather only one of the latest phases of its evolution." Methodologically, from the point of view of studying nonbelief—specifically through the lens of sociology, which is so rooted in the study of religion—the issue is how to go about studying nonbelief in its specificity, on the one hand, while noting its interaction with religion, on the other. While scholars—including ourselves—have rightly noted the relationship between the two, it's important not to unreflexively assume that the methods used to study religion necessarily suffice to study nonbelief. To the extent that such studies do not seek to address nonbelief as a phenomenon in its own right—but treat it as a defensive response, or as a "deviant" epiphenomenon—then such studies cannot help but promote the view that nonbelief, and all that entails in terms of institutions and individuals, is a derivative component of our contemporary social landscape. In attempting to let secularists speak for themselves throughout significant portions of our book, we have at least attempted to be fair in this regard—taking seriously secularists as individuals and secularism as a social movement.

APPENDIX 2

Survey 1 was used for research included in chapter 2 on the new atheism and revised to ask more questions about the Internet and atheism for research included in Chapter 3. Note that with all the surveys, respondents were given space to write out their thoughts in addition to or as opposed to merely checking an answer. Some used this option to critique the questions or the way in which the questions were composed.

1) Have you read the books/documentaries by the so-called new atheists? Which ones?
2) Which is your favorite? Why?
3) Which is your least favorite? Why?
4) Has reading these books or watching such a film as *Religulous* changed your views or understandings of atheism?

    a) Yes
    b) No

5) If so, in what ways have your own views changed?
6) Has the fact that these books are bestsellers and are widely featured in the media given you a greater sense of acceptance or support in society?

    a) Yes
    b) No

7) Do you think reading these books and/or watching this film has changed theists' views and ideas about atheism and atheists in a more favorable or less favorable direction?

    a) More favorable
    b) Less favorable
    c) No change

8) Because of these books/films and their popular reception, are you more likely or less likely to say you are an atheist? Or has there been no change?

   a) More likely
   b) Less likely
   c) No change

9) If you answered less likely in the last question, is there another designation you have used to describe your views since the new atheist phenomenon started? If so, what is this designation?

10) Have you recommended these books to friends, colleagues, family members who are not atheists/secular humanists?

   a) Yes
   b) No

11) Have you noticed new people becoming involved in your particular humanist group since these books/film have been published/released?

   a) Yes
   b) No

12) Has your particular humanist organization recommended or studied these books as a group?

   a) Yes
   b) No

13) Does the Internet inform your atheism? If so, how?

14) The media has made much of the "nasty" attitude of new atheism (causing some secular groups to distinguish themselves from "this type of atheism" in print and online). Do you have any opinions on this?

15) In conclusion, how do you think these books and the film will affect the perception of atheists/secular humanists in the United States?

Survey 2 was used for research included in chapter 4 on secularist rituals and commemorations.

1) There has been a move by some atheists to emphasize a more positive identity and take a more conciliatory stance toward religious believers. What do you think of this idea about putting less priority on "debunking" and criticizing religion?

   a) Agree
   b) Disagree

Comment:

2) It has also been suggested that rituals, such as rites of passage (including weddings, coming-of-age ceremonies, funerals), need to be given more attention in secularist groups. What is your opinion regarding this proposal?

    a) Agree
    b) Disagree

Comment:

3) Have you ever participated in these kinds of rituals within, or sponsored by, an organized secular group? If so, what was the occasion?

    a) Yes
    b) No

Comment:

4) If you have not participated in such rituals, would you be open to such participation?

    a) Yes
    b) No

Comment:

5) If you have participated in such rituals, was this experience favorable or not?

    a) Favorable
    b) Unfavorable
    c) Neither favorable nor unfavorable

Comment:

6) If it was favorable, would you want such ceremonies to have a more regular part in your atheist or secular humanist group?

    a) Yes
    b) No

Comment:

7) Often people who are involved in religious rituals feel a sense of community by their participation. Have you ever had a similar feeling from secular ceremonies or rituals?

    a) Yes
    b) No

Comment:

8) How about such feelings of awe and wonder or being connected with the universe? Have you ever had any of these feelings from participation in secular rituals or ceremonies?

   a) Yes
   b) No

Comment:

9) Some have defined the above feelings as comprising a "secular spirituality" (not involving a supernatural entity). Have you ever had these feelings from other activities? Please check those activities where you have experienced these feelings.

   a) Being in or observing nature
   b) Reading about or working in science
   c) Using technology for life enhancement or extension
   d) Social or political activism
   e) Listening to/performing music
   f) Admiring/doing art
   g) Playing sports/exercise
   h) Childbirth/child-raising/ family relations
   i) Sexual activity
   j) Friendship/social activities
   k) Working

Comment:

NOTES

Chapter 1

1. As a case in point, religious movements are more and more forced to use secular terminology in presenting and defending their claims in the public sphere. In the push for creation to be taught in public schools, for example, they must argue that it is consistent with scientific evidence (a point that helps explain the use of the terms "*intelligent* design" or "creation *science*"). When it comes to abortion, they must oppose it on the grounds that it violates the right to life. And when it comes to divorce, it is described as dysfunctional, as opposed to disapproved by God. In short, when advocating and presenting their cause in the court of law and the court of public opinion, religious activists are forced to argue and defend their point in legal and secular terms.
2. Not all secularists agree on this point, however. For example, when asking about the status of secularism in the United States, one response we received was, "What status? We are such a nonvocal minority. I hope more people will start speaking up. But President Obama isn't helping with keeping faith-based initiatives in the White House and all the 'god bless America' stuff."
3. Note that the mission statement as quoted has been modified and can be found at http://secularpartyofamerica.tumblr.com/, which is the current homepage. It now reads as follows:

    The Secular Party of America seeks to politically represent U.S. atheists and all who share the goal of a secular government by gathering the political strength of secularists nationwide while being guided by the values of secular humanism and evidenced-based reasoning.

4. A more scholarly subtitle to our book would have been "from separation to equality." Secularists—in moving from the margins to the center—are not just looking to protect their version of the wall of separation; they are looking for actual equality and legitimization. Examples include atheists seeking their own chaplains, their own bedside care in hospitals and burial rites, and their own wedding ceremonies, as well as the vocal call for atheists to move into political and cultural society to a stronger degree—even going so far to start the aforementioned "political party." Given the increase in the secular, or at least non-affiliated, population (see Amor 1998), and the Supreme Court's increasing tendency to "shy away from aggressively applying the religion clauses to the states" (Payne 2013), the use of the establishment clause to defend the influence of religion may become less successful in some states. If this happens we may see atheists following the gay and civil rights movements in using equal-protection arguments, such as recently filed in Massachusetts.

Chapter 2

1. McGrath (2013) more recently argued that the new atheism is a "populist splinter group" within atheism; in contrast, we see it as having a much greater impact within secularism.
2. Dawkins 2007; Dennett 2006; Harris 2004; Hitchens 2007b.
3. The majority/minority distinction in this case has less to do with sheer numbers than with the fact that theism arguably remains the normative standard in comparison to which nontheism can be said to be minority in the United States. In spite of the fact that "America," as Peter Berger is quick to point out, "is less religious than it seems because it has a cultural elite which is heavily secularized" (Mathewes 2006: 155). Of course, these same cultural elites would appear, more often than not, to find publicly professing to a belief in God to be advantageous, at least in the political sphere. This is not as surprising as it might initially seem, perhaps, when one considers that secularism and Enlightenment thought came to the United States supported by religion rather than at its expense (Casanova 2006; Himmelfarb 2004).
4. This quote is from the press release for Kurtz's paper, "What Is Secular Humanism?," available at www.secularhumanism.org. The ousting of Kurtz as chairman of CFI in the summer of 2009 has been reported as signaling a changing of the guard in the organization toward a more aggressive atheist position. See Button 2010.
5. This is supported by our content analysis of elite and popular media in chapter 3.

Chapter 3

1. The authors conducted textual analysis of the *New York Times'* coverage of atheism specifically in three decades, the 1920s, the 1960s, and 2000s (although articles in subsequent decades also were included for examination). We also examined the *Washington Post*, analyzing 150 articles from 1989 to 2013. The coverage prior to and after the emergence of new atheism, around 2006, was given special attention.

2. See Shweder 2006.

3. For further views on a defense of new atheism along similar lines, see Schulzke 2013.

4. Women continue to be largely overlooked in contemporary atheism and secular history/studies, even though they have been behind many great secular accomplishments. Debbie Goddard, for example, founded the African Americans for Humanism (AAH), and Sergeant Kathleen Johnson, an Iraq War veteran, founded the Military Association of Atheists and Freethinkers (MAAF). There's also the case of Susan Jacoby being overlooked as playing a part in new atheism and secular studies, particularly with respect to her work on the history of secularity in the United States. See the *Free Inquiry* December 2012/January 2013 issue for some interesting articles on "Women in Secularism."

5. Our reference here is to cultural capital as understood by Pierre Bourdieu. For an introduction to Bourdieu's concept of capital, see Moore 2008.

6. The vanguard here is not conceived as an intellectual wing of a party or movement, but as the vanguard within society as a whole, fueled by the desire to educate the religious masses and protect the secular state from religious influence.

7. Research shows that secularists, on average, tend to be generally well off economically (Stark 2008). The issue of class is still a largely neglected area of research within the growing body of secularity studies. And although we haven't dealt with the issue of class here, more and more articles and posts online are discussing the issue from various angles. For starters, see Hoelscher 2012.

8. We don't see the heuristic use of making a hard distinction between subcultures and movements. Most movements have and express subcultural tendencies in terms of forming oppositional symbols and messages and forming counterpublics. As Laura Olson (2011) convincingly argues, the concept of subculture is largely latent in social movement approaches. Moreover, both approaches, when worked in tandem, can help highlight the dual-sidedness (defensive and assertive) of movements. Further, both approaches, especially with the rise of identity politics and a move away from strictly economic and redistributive concerns, share a concern over the effectiveness of cultural politics (Martin 2002). If there is a disagreement with the use of subculture for us, it is with the essentialism that has accompanied its use in the past. Secularists in particular do not

express a unified style. Philosophically, the secularist movement and commu-nity are much closer to Jean-Luc Nancy's notion of an inoperative community or Maffesoli's neo-tribes than a subculture in its past conceptualizations.

9. While we feel that Williamson and Yancey are largely correct in their political assessment of American atheists being aligned to a political agenda that sits firmly left of center and are "progressive," especially among the young, we feel that a few issues throw the whole "progressive" notion into question. First and foremost, there is the strong libertarian streak that runs throughout the movement, which clearly aligns some atheists with a politics that supports fiscal conservativism and a free-market approach regarding economic issues. Additionally, and related, there is the utter lack of even a hint of a critique of free-market capitalism—long a staple of what is typically taken as progressive politics—emanating from the center of the atheist movement in the United States. When you couple this with the Darwinian framework—which has been used and abused by conservatives, starting from Herbert Spencer, to justify their politics—that informs some of the public atheist intellectuals' work (and trickles down to the grass roots in some form), we feel that fur-ther research is needed to fully align atheists as a whole with any particular political agenda or party. In short, defining what an atheist politics might look like is difficult because its political identity is so ambiguous. Atheists don't like to be lumped into categories. We think it's safe to say the majority are *socially* liberal and support the separation of church and state. But beyond that, we believe that things get slightly more nuanced and complex, as they likely would when looking to align closely any social identity group to a par-ticular political persuasion. Perhaps Greg Laden (2012: 30) put it best: "We are mostly a progressive movement, even though we also reach out to more conservative factions and there are plenty of Republicans, libertarians, and other nonprogressives in the movement."

Chapter 4

1. We would like to thank Ayako Sairenji for her observation of the Darwin Day in New Jersey.

REFERENCES

Adler, Jerry. 2007. "Blasphemy." *Newsweek*, January 8.

Aikman, David. 2008. *The Delusion of Disbelief.* Wheaton, IL: Tyndale.

Allen, Norm. 2007. "In Defense of Radicalism." *Free Inquiry*, 27:4, June/July: 52.

Amarasingam, Amarath, ed. 2010. *The New Atheism.* Leiden: Brill.

Amor, Abdelfattah. 1998. "Special Rapporteur on the Question of Religious Intolerance, Civil and Political Rights." New York: United Nations Commission on Human Rights.

Angier, Natalie. 2001. "Confessions of a Lonely Atheist," *New York Times,* January 14.

Anderson, Benedict. 1991. *Imagined Communities: Reflections on the Origin and Spread of Nationalism.* New York: Verso.

Anne. 2013. "National Atheist Party Drops the Name 'Atheist'." What Would JT Do? Blog, http://www.patheos.com/blogs/wwjtd/2013/07/national-atheist-party-drops-the-name-atheist/.

Asad, Talal. 2002. *Formations of the Secular: Christianity, Islam, and Modernity.* Palo Alto, CA: Stanford University Press.

Baggini, Julian. 2007. "Toward a More Mannerly Secularism." *Free Inquiry*, 27:2, February/March: 41–44.

Bainbridge, William Sims. 2005. "Atheism." *Interdisciplinary Journal of Research on Religion,* 1:2: 36–44.

Beit-Hallahmi, Benjamin. 2007. "Atheists: A Psychological Profile." In *The Cambridge Companion to Atheism*, ed. Michael Martin. New York: Cambridge University Press. 300–317.

Berger, Peter. 2013. "Angry Atheists." Religion and Other Curiosities blog, http://blogs.the.american-interest.com/berger/2013/07/17/angry-atheists/.

Berger, Peter, ed. 1999. *The Desecularization of the World.* Grand Rapids: Eerdmans.

Berkman, M. B., J. S. Pacheco, and E. Plutzer. 2008. "Evolution and Creationism in America's Classrooms: A National Portrait." *PLoS Biology*, 6:5: e124. doi:10.1371/journal.pbio.0060124.

Bernstein, Mary. 1997. "Celebration and Suppression: The Strategic Uses of Identity by the Lesbian and Gay Movement." *American Journal of Sociology*, 103:3: 531–565.

Bice, J. 2007. "Taking Atheism out of the Closet." *American Atheist*, August: 21–23.

Borer, Michael Ian. 2010. "The New Atheism and the Secularization Thesis." In *Religion and the New Atheism*, ed. Amarnath Amarasingam. Leiden: Brill. 125–137.

Bruce, Steve. 2002. *God Is Dead: Secularization in the West*. Malden: MA: Blackwell.

Budd, Susan. 1977. *Varieties of Unbelief*. London: Heinemann.

Bullivant, Stephen. 2010. "The New Atheism and Sociology" In *Religion and the New Atheism*, ed. Amarnath Amarasingam. Leiden: Brill. 109–124.

Bullivant, Stephen. 2012. "Not So Indifferent After All? Self-Conscious Atheism and the Secularization Thesis." *Approaching Religion*, 2:1, June: 100–106.

Button, Thea. 2010. "The Fighting Atheists." *Religion in the News*, 11, Winter, http://www.trincoll.edu/idents/csrpl.

Calhoun, Craig. 1992. *Habermas and the Public Sphere*. Cambridge, MA: MIT Press.

Campbell, Colin. 1972. *The Sociology of Irreligion*. New York: Herder and Herder.

Campbell, David. 2013. "The Politics of Irreligion." Paper presented at Institute for Religion Culture and Public Life seminar, Columbia University, New York, October 17.

Carpignano, Paolo. 1999. "The Shape of the Sphere: The Public Sphere and the Materiality of Communication." *Constellations*, 6:2, June: 177–189.

Carpignano, Paolo, Robin Andersen, Stanley Aronowitz, and William DiFazio. 1993. "Chatter in the Age of Electronic Reproduction: Talk Television and the 'Public Mind.'" In *The Phantom Public Sphere*, ed. Bruce Robbins. Minneapolis: University of Minnesota Press. 93–120.

Carroll, John. 2011. "Beauty Contra God: Has Aesthetics Replaced Religion in Modernity?" *Journal of Sociology*, online first version, August 3: 1–18.

Casanova, Jose. 1994. *Public Religions in the Modern World*. Chicago: University of Chicago Press.

Casanova, Jose. 2006. "Secularism Revisited: A Reply to Talal Asad." In *Powers of the Secular Modern: Talal Asad and His Interlocutors*, ed. David Scott and Charles Hirschkind. Stanford, CA: Stanford University Press. 12–30.

Castells, Manuel. 1997. *The Power of Identity*. Oxford: Blackwell.

Chesterton, Gilbert Keith. 1963. *The Ball and the Cross*. Beaconsfield: Darwin Finlayson Ltd.

Christina, Greta. 2013. "What Does Religion Provide?" *Free Inquiry*, 33:3, April/May: 8.

Cimino, Richard. 2011. "Informatic Futurists Borrowing and Targeting Religion, and Gaining New Credibility." *Religion Watch*, 26:5, July–August: 3.

Cimino, Richard. 2012. "Current Research." *Religion Watch*, 27:3, March/April: 5.

Cimino, Richard, and Christopher Smith. 2007. "Secular Humanism and Atheism Beyond Progressive Secularism." *Sociology of Religion*, 68:4, Winter: 407–424.

Cimino, Richard, and Christopher Smith. 2011. "The New Atheism and the Formation of the Imagined Secularist Community." *Journal of Media and Religion*, 10:4, January/March: 24–38.

Cipolla, Benedicta. 2007. "Is Atheism Just a Rant Against Religion?" *Washington Post*, May 26.

Cline, Austin. 2010. "Weekly Poll: Are So-Called 'New Atheists' Too Assertive or Not Assertive Enough?" About.com, http://atheism.about.com/b/2010/07/22/weekly-poll-are-so-called-new-atheists-too-assertive-or-not-assertive-enough.htm.

Collins, Randall. 2010. "The Micro-Sociology of Religion: Religious Practices, Collective and Individual." The ARDA Guiding Paper Series, http://www.thearda.com.

Cowan, Douglas E. 2013. "And Take Your Invisible Friends with You." *Bulletin for the Study of Religion*, 42:3, September: 32–36.

Cragun, Ryan. 2012. "Who Are the New Atheists?" Paper presented at the Consultation on Atheism, Canadian Research Council University of Ottawa, Ontario, November 22–24.

Cragun, Ryan, Stephanie Yeager, and Desmond Vega. 2012. "Research Report: How Secular Humanists (and Everyone Else) Subsidize Religion in the United States." *Free Inquiry*, 32:4, June/July: 39–46.

Dart, John. 2001. "Churchgoers from Elsewhere." *Christian Century*, December 15, 8–9.

Davie, Grace. 2004. "New Approaches in the Sociology of Religion: A Western Perspective." *Social Compass*, 51: 73–84.

Davis, Richard. 2009. *Typing Politics: The Role of Blogs in American Politics.* New York: Oxford University Press.

Dawkins, Richard. 2003. "Now Here's an Idea." *Free Inquiry,* 23:4, October/November: 12–13.

Dawkins, Richard. 2006. *The God Delusion.* New York: Houghton-Mifflin.

Dawkins, Richard. 2007. "Science and the New Atheism." *Point of Inquiry* podcast, December 7, http://www.pointofinquiry.org/richard_dawkins_science_and_the_new_atheism.

De Botton, Alain. 2012. *Religion for Atheists: A Nonbeliever's Guide to the Uses of Religion.* New York: Pantheon.

Dennett, Daniel. 2006. *Breaking the Spell.* New York: Viking.

Diani, Mario. 2000. "Social Movement Networks Virtual and Real." *Information, Communication and Society*, 3:3: 386–401.

DMCAabuse. 2008. "Creationist DMCA Abuse." YouTube, http://www.youtube.com/DMCAabuse#p/u/11/aWZ9XcdbO0w.

Eder, Klaus. 1993. *The New Politics of Class: Social Movements and Cultural Dynamics in Advanced Societies*. London: Sage.

Edgell, Penny, Joseph Gerteis, and Douglas Hartmann. 2006. "Atheists as 'Other': Moral Boundaries and Cultural Membership in American Society." *American Sociological Review*, 71, April: 674–687.

Epstein, Greg M. 2009a. *Good Without God*. New York: William Morrow.

Epstein, Greg M. 2009b. "Why the New Humanism?" *The New Humanism*, http://www.thenewhumanism.org/authors/greg-epstein/articles/why-the-new-humanism.

Farley, Tim. 2009. "Skepticism via YouTube." Committee for Skeptical Inquiry, http://www.csicop.org/si/show/skepticism_via_youtube/.

Farred, Grant. 2000. "Endgame Identity? Mapping the New Left Roots of Identity Politics." *New Literary History*, 31:4, Autumn: 627–648.

Flynn, Tom. 2002. "Drawing the Boundaries: Humanism—Secular and Religious." *Free Inquiry*, 22:4, Fall: 35–43.

Flynn, Tom. 2005. "Glimpses of Nirvana." *Free Inquiry*, 25:2, February/March: 53–54.

Flynn, Tom. 2012a. "Does Secular Humanism Have a Political Agenda?" *Free Inquiry*, 32:6, October/November: 18.

Flynn, Tom. 2012b. "Good Without God (Review)." *Free Inquiry*, 30:2, February/March: 57.

Flynn, Tom. 2013. "Is Religion Dying?" *Free Inquiry*, 33:4, June/July: 201.

Fox, Jonathan. 2014. "Is It Really God's Century?" *Politics and Religion*, 7:1, March: 4–27.

Fraser, Nancy. 1992. "Rethinking the Public Sphere: A Contribution to the Critique of Actual Existing Democracy." In *Habermas and the Public Sphere*, ed. Craig Calhoun. Cambridge, MA: MIT Press. 104–142.

Freethought Kampala. 2011. "Elevatorgate." http://freethoughtkampala.wordpress.com/2011/09/11/elevatorgate/

Funk, Cary, Greg Smith, and Luis Lugo. 2012. " 'Nones' on the Rise." Washington, DC: Pew Research Center, http://www.pewforum.org/2012/10/09/nones-on-the-rise/.

Galen, Luke. 2009. "Profiles of the Godless: Results from a Survey of the Non-Religious." *Free Inquiry*, 29:5, August/September: 41–45.

Gamson, Joshua. 1997. "Messages of Exclusion: Gender, Movements, and Symbolic Boundaries." *Gender and Society*, 11:2, April: 178–199.

Gamson, William A., and David S. Meyer. 1996. "Framing Political Opportunity." In *Comparative Perspectives on Social Movements: Political Opportunities, Mobilizing Structures, and Cultural Framings*, ed. Doug McAdam, John D. McCarthy, and Mayer N. Zald. Cambridge: Cambridge University Press. 275–290.

Garcia, Alfredo, and Joseph Blankholm. 2013. "The Social Context of Active Disbelief: County-Level Predictors of Disbelief Organizations in the United States." Paper presented at the meeting of the Association for the Sociology of Religion, New York, August 10–12.

Geertz, Clifford. 1973. *Interpretation of Cultures*. New York: Basic Books.

Goffman, Erving. 1963. *Stigma: Notes on the Management of Spoiled Identity*. New York: Prentice-Hall.

Goldberg, Michelle. 2007. *Kingdom Coming: The Rise of Christian Nationalism*. New York: W. W. Norton.

Goldberg, Rachel Tillie. 2009. "Counterpublics and Media Policing: Atheism and the Challenge to Public Sphere Boundaries." Ph.D. dissertation, University of Washington.

Goldfarb, Jeffrey C. 2001. "1989 and the Creativity of the Political." *Social Research*, 68:4, Summer: 993–1010.

Goldfarb, Jeffrey C. 2009. "On Barack Obama." *Constellations*, 16:2, June 2: 235–250.

Goodstein, Laurie. 2009. "More Atheists Are Shouting It from Rooftops." *New York Times*, April 29.

Graeber, David. 2011. *Possibilities: Essays on Hierarchy, Rebellion, and Desire*. Oakland: AK Press.

Gramsci, Antonio. 1971. *Selections from the Prison Notebooks*. London: Lawrence and Wishart.

Granovetter, Mark S. 1973. "The Strength of Weak Ties." *American Journal of Sociology*, 78:6, May: 1360–1380.

Grothe, Douglas James, and Austin Dacey. 2004. "Atheism Is Not a Civil Rights Issue." *Free Inquiry*, 24:2, March, http:www.secularhumanism.org.

Guadia, G. 2008. "God Is Not Great." *American Atheist*, September: 29–30.

Habermas, Jürgen. 1989. *The Structural Transformation of the Public Sphere: An Inquiry into a Category of Bourgeois Society*. Cambridge, MA: MIT Press.

Hadaway, Christopher Kirk, et al. 1993. "What the Polls Don't Show: A Closer Look at U.S. Church Attendance." *American Sociological Review*, 58:6, December: 741–752.

Hansen, Susan B. 2011. *Religion and Reaction*. Lanham, MD: Rowman and Littlefield.

Harris, Sam. 2004. *The End of Faith: Religion, Terror, and the Future of Reason*. New York: W. W. Norton.

Harris, Sam. 2007. "The Problem with Atheism." Presentation at the Atheist Alliance conference, Washington, DC, September 28.

Hart, Roderick P. 1978. "An Unquiet Desperation: Rhetorical Aspects of 'Popular' Atheism in the United States." *Quarterly Journal of Speech*, 64:1: 33–46.

Hedges, Chris. 2008. *I Don't Believe in Atheists*. New York: Free Press.

Himmelfarb, Gertrude. 2004. *The Roads to Modernity*. New York: Knopf.

Hitchens, Christopher. 2007a. "Bullshitting About Atheism." *Free Inquiry*, 27:4, June/July: 24–25.

Hitchens, Christopher. 2007b. *God Is Not Great*. New York: Warner Books.

Hoelscher, David. 2012. "Atheism and the Class Problem." *CounterPunch,* November 7, http://www.counterpunch.org/2012/11/07/atheism-and-the-class-problem/#.UJyJXmTZcH8.facebook.

Hoffmann, R. J. 2006. "Spiritual Libertarians." *Free Inquiry*, 25:6, October/November: 25–27.

Hooper, Simon. 2006. "The Rise of the 'New Atheists.'" CNN, http://edition.cnn.com/2006/WORLD/europe/11/08/atheism.feature/index.html.

Hout, Michael, and Claude Fischer. 2002. "Why More Americans Have No Religious Preference: Politics and Generations." *American Sociological Review*, 65, April: 165–190.

Humanist Manifesto 2000. 1999. *Free Inquiry*, 20:1, Winter: 6.

Humanist Manifestos I and II. 1973. Buffalo, NY: Prometheus Books.

Hunsberger, Bruce E., and Bob Altemeyer. 2006. *Atheists: A Groundbreaking Study of America's Nonbelievers*. Amherst, NY: Prometheus Books.

Innis, Harold. 1984. *The Bias of Communication*. Toronto: University of Toronto Press.

Jacoby, Susan. 2004. *Freethinkers*. New York: Metropolitan Books.

Jasper, James. 2010. "Strategic Marginalizations, Emotional Marginalities: The Dilemma of Stigmatized Identities." In *Surviving Against Odds*, ed. Debal K. SinghaRoy. New Delhi, India: Manohar Publishers. 29–37.

Keysar, Ariela, Egon Mayer, and Barry A. Kosmin. 2003. *No Religion: A Profile of America's Unaffiliated*. Hartford, CT: Institute for the Study of Secularism in Society and Culture.

Koch, Gretchen. 2008. "Full of Sound and Fury: The Media Response to Dennett." *Method and Theory in the Study of Religion*, 20: 36-44.

Koepsell, David. 2007. "Humanism and Civil Rights." *Free Inquiry*, 25:6, October/November: 16.

Kosmin, Barry A., and Ariela Keysar. 2009. *American Nones: The Profile of the No Religion Population*. Hartford, CT: Institute for the Study of Secularism in Society and Culture.

Kosmin, Barry A., and Ariela Keysar, eds. 2007. *Secularism and Secularity*. Hartford, CT: Institute for the Study of Secularism in Society and Culture.

Kunda, Ziva. 1999. *Social Cognition: Making Sense of People*. Cambridge, MA: MIT Press.

Kurtz, Paul. 2000. "The Need to Come out of the Closet." *Free Inquiry*, 20:3, Summer: 5–6.

Kurtz, Paul. 2002. "Are Science and Religion Compatible?" *Skeptical Inquirer*, March/April, http://www.csicop.org/si/.

Kurtz, Paul. 2007a. "Are 'Evangelical Atheists' Too Outspoken?" *Free Inquiry*, 27:2, February/March: 4–5.

Kurtz, Paul. 2007b. "The New Atheism and Secular Humanism." *Point of Inquiry* podcast, September 14, http://www.pointofinquiry.org/paul_kurtz_the_new_atheism_and_secular_humanism/.

Kurtz, Paul. 2007c. "'Yes' to Naturalism, Secularism, and Humanism." *Free Inquiry*, 27:3, April/May: 4–5.

Kurtz, Paul. 2008. "Secular Humanist Convictions." *Secular Humanist Bulletin*, 24:1: 2.

Laden, Greg. 2012. "Secularism's Place in Politics." *Free Inquiry*, 32:6, October/November: 28–30.

LaHaye, Tim. 1984. *The Battle for the Mind.* Grand Rapids: Baker Book House.

LaHaye, Tim, and David Noebel. 2000. *Mind Siege.* Nashville: Word.

Lamont, Corliss. 1990. *The Philosophy of Humanism.* New York: Continuum.

Lawton, Graham. 2012. "The God Issue: Alain de Botton's Religion for Atheists." *New Scientist*, 2856, March: http://www.newscientist.com

LeDrew, Stephen. 2012. "The Evolution of Atheism: Scientific and Humanistic Approaches." *History of the Human Sciences*, 25:3, July: 70–87.

LeDrew, Stephen. 2013. "Discovering Atheism: Heterogeneity in Trajectories to Atheist Identity and Activism." *Sociology of Religion*, 74:2, Summer: 1–24.

Levitt, Norman. 2001. "The Sources and Dangers of Postmodern Anti-Science." *Free Inquiry*, 21:2, Spring: 24.

Lindsey, Michael. 2007. *Faith in the Halls of Power: How Evangelicals Joined the American Elite.* New York: Oxford University Press.

Loxton, Daniel. 2009. "The Paradoxical Future of Skepticism." *Skeptical Inquirer*, November/December: 24–27.

Lyall, Sarah. 2009. "Atheists Decide to Send Their Own Message, on 800 Buses." *New York Times*, January 7.

Lyotard, Jean-François. 1984. *The Postmodern Condition: A Report on Knowledge.* Minneapolis: University of Minnesota Press.

Marshall, David. 2007. *The Truth Behind the New Atheism.* Eugene, OR: Harvest House Publishers.

Martin, Greg. 2002. "Conceptualising Cultural Politics in Subcultural and Social Movements Studies." *Social Movement Studies: Journal of Social, Cultural and Political Protest*, 1:1: 73–88.

Marty, Martin E. 1961. *The Infidel: Freethought and American Religion*: Cleveland: Meridian Books.

Marx, Karl. 1978. "A Contribution to the Critique of Hegel's Philosophy of Right: Introduction." In *The Marx-Engels Reader*, 2nd ed., ed. Robert C. Tucker. New York: W . W. Norton. 53–65.

Mathewes, Charles T. 2006. "An Interview with Peter Berger." *Hedgehog Review*, 8:1–2, Spring/Summer: 152–161.

McAdam, Doug, Sidney Tarrow, and Charles Tilly. 2001. *Dynamics of Contention.* Cambridge: Cambridge University Press.

McGrath, Alister. 2004. *The Twilight of Atheism.* New York: Doubleday.

McGrath, Alister. 2007. *The Dawkins Delusion* (with Joanna Collicutt McGrath). London: SPCK Publishers.

McGrath, Alister. 2013. "Evidence, Theory, and Interpretation: The `New Atheism' and the Philosophy of Science." *Midwest Studies in Philosophy*, XXXVII: 178–188.

McGrath, Peter. 2012. "Is American Atheism Headed for a Schism?" *The Guardian*, September 2, http://www.theguardian.com.

McLuhan, Marshall. 1964. *Understanding Media: The Extensions of Man.* London: Routledge.

Mehta, Hemant. 2009. "Would You Be an Atheist Without the Internet?" *Friendly Atheist*, http://www.patheos.com/blogs/friendatheist.

Merino, S. M. 2012. "Irreligious Socialization? The Adult Religious Preferences of Individuals Raised with No Religion." *Secularism and Nonreligion* 1: 1–16, http://dx.doi.org/10.5334/snr.aa.

Meyrowitz, Joshua. 1985. *No Sense of Place: The Impact of Electronic Media on Social Behavior.* New York: Oxford University Press.

Meyrowitz, Joshua. 1994. "Medium Theory." In *Communication Theory Today*, ed. David Crowley and David Mitchell. Stanford, CA: Stanford University Press. 50–77.

Meyrowitz, Joshua. 2000. "Multiple Media Literacies." In *Television: The Critical View*, ed. Horace Newcomb. New York: Oxford University Press. 425–438.

Meyrowitz, Joshua, and John Maguire. 1993. "Media, Place, and Multiculturalism." *Society*, 30:5, July/August: 41–48.

Miller, Ashley. 2013. "The Non-Religious Patriarchy: Why Losing Religion Has Not Meant Losing White Male Dominance." *CrossCurrents*, 63:2: 211–226.

Mohler, Richard Albert. 2008. *Atheism Remix*. Wheaton, IL: Crossway

Moore, Robert. 2008. "Capital." In *Pierre Bourdieu: Key Concepts*, ed. Michael Grenfell. North Yorkshire, UK: Acumen. 101–117.

Murray, Douglas. 2013. "Richard Dawkins Interview." *The Spectator*, September 14, http://www.spectator.co.uk.

Muscato, Dave. 2013. "Thank You, R/Atheism from the Bottom of My Soul (If I Had One)." Reddit, March 22, http://www.reddit.com/r/atheism/comments1auidv/thank_you_ratheism.

Myers, Paul Zachary. 2010. "Witless Wanker Peddles Pablum for CFI." Pharyngula blog, http://scienceblogs.com/pharyngula/2010/04/witless_wanker_peddles_pablum.php.

Myers, Paul Zachary. 2011a. "A Common Atheist Delusion." Freethought Blogs: Pharyngula, December 14, http://freethoughtblogs.com/pharyngula/2011/12/14/a-common-atheist-delusion/.

Myers, Paul Zachary. 2011b. "Atheist Church? NO THANK YOU." Freethought Blogs: Pharyngula, October 17, http://freethoughtblogs.com/pharyngula/2011/10/17/atheist-church-no-thank-you/.

Myers, Paul Zachary. 2012. "I'm Officially Disgusted with Alain de Botton." Freethought Blogs: Pharyngula, February 28, http://freethoughtblogs.com/pharyngula/2012/02/28/i-am-officially-disgusted-with-alain-de-botton/.

Nabors, Bradly. 2009. "The Changing Forms of Organized Nonbelief: The Case of the Pacific City Atheists." Paper presented at the Association for the Sociology of Religion meeting, San Francisco, August.

Nanda, Meera. 2008. "Trading Faith for Spirituality." *American Atheist*, February: 20–25.

National Center for Science Education. 2013. "Chronology of 'Academic Freedom' Bills." http://ncse.com/creationism/general/chronology-academic-freedom-bills, September 7.

Negt, Oskar, and Alexander Kluge. 1993. *Public Sphere and Experience: Toward an Analysis of the Bourgeois and Proletarian Public Sphere.* Minneapolis: University of Minnesota Press.

Nepstad, Sharon Erikson, and Christian Smith. 1999. "Rethinking Recruitment to High-Risk/Cost Activism: The Case of Nicaragua Exchange." *Mobilization*, 4:1, April: 25–40.

Nickerson, Raymond S. 1998. "Confirmation Bias: A Ubiquitous Phenomenon in Many Guises." *Review of General Psychology*, 2:2: 175–220.

Nietzsche, Friedrich. 1967. *On the Genealogy of Morals and Ecce Homo.* New York: Vintage.

Niose, David. 2012. *Nonbeliever Nation.* New York: Palgrave Macmillan.

Nisbet, Matthew. 2007. "Atheism Is Not a Civil Rights Issue." Framing Science blog, June 28, http://scienceblogs.com/framing-science/2007/06/28/atheism-is-not-a-civil-rights/.

Norris, Pippa, and Ronald Inglehart. 2004. *Sacred and Secular: Religion and Politics Worldwide.* New York: Cambridge University Press.

Novak, Michael. 2008. *No One Sees God: The Dark Night of Atheists and Believers.* New York: Doubleday.

Olson, Laura. 2011. "The Essentiality of 'Culture' in the Study of Religion and Politics." *Journal for the Scientific Study of Religion*, 50:4, December: 639–653.

Ormerod, Neil. 2010. "Secularisation and the 'Rise' of Atheism." *Australian Journal of Theology*, 17: 13–22.

Oswald, Margit E., and Stefan Grosjean. 2004. "Confirmation Bias." In *Cognitive Illusions: A Handbook on Fallacies and Biases in Thinking, Judgement, and Memory*, ed. Rüdiger F. Pohl. Hove, UK: Psychology Press. 79–96.

Pasquale, Frank. 2010. "A Portrait of Secular Group Affiliates." In *Atheism and Secularity*, vol. 1, ed. Phil Zuckerman. Santa Barbara, CA: Prager. 43–47.

Payne, Alan. 2013. "Redefining 'Atheism' in America: What the United States Could Learn from Europe's Protection of Atheists." *Emory International Law Review*, 27:1.: 663–703.

Perkins, Greg. 2008. "Why the New Atheists Can't Even Beat D'Souza: The Best and Worst in Human History." Diana Hsieh: NoodleFood blog, May 20, http://www.dianahsieh.com/blog/2008/05/why-new-atheists-cant-even-beat-dsouza.shtml?nc.

Perl, Paul, and Richard Cimino. 2011. "The Role of Church-State Conflict in the Vitality of Secular Activism and Membership." Unpublished paper.

Pew Research Center. 2012. "'Nones' on the Rise." http://www.pewforum.org/2012/10/09/nones-on-the-rise/.

Pigliucci, Massimo. 2008. "Is Dawkins Deluded?" *American Atheist,* May/June: 16–18.

Pigliucci, Massimo. 2010a. "PZ Myers Is a Witless Wanker Who Peddles Pablum." Rationally Speaking blog, http://rationallyspeaking.blogspot.com/2010/04/pz-myers-is-witless-wanker-who-peddles.html

Pigliucci, Massimo. 2010b. "The Scientific Study of Religion." Rationally Speaking blog http://rationallyspeaking.blogspot.com/2010/10/scientific-study-of-religion.html

Polletta, Francesca. 1999. "Free Spaces in Collective Action." *Theory and Society.* 28:1: 1–38.

Poster, Mark. 1996. "Cyberdemocracy: Internet and the Public Sphere." In *Internet Culture,* ed. David Porter. New York: Routledge. 201–217.

Quattrone, George A., and Amos Tversky. 1988. "Contrasting Rational and Psychological Analyses of Political Choice." *American Political Science Review,* 82:3, August: 719–736.

Roof, Wade Clark. 1999. *Spiritual Marketplace.* Princeton, NJ: Princeton University Press.

Sandler, Lauren. 2006. *Righteous: Dispatches from the Evangelical Youth Movement.* New York: Penguin.

Schulzke, Marcus. 2013. "The Politics of the New Atheism." *Politics and Religion,* 6:4, December: 778–799.

Shermer, Michael. 1999. *How We Believe: The Search for God in an Age of Science.* New York: Freeman.

Shermer, Michael. 2003. "The Big 'Bright' Brouhaha: An Empirical Study on an Emerging Skeptical Movement." *Skeptic,* 10:3, http://www.skeptic.com.

Shweder, Richard A. 2006. "Atheists Agonistes." *New York Times,* November 27.

Silk, Mark. 1995. *Unsecular Media.* Urbana: University of Illinois Press.

Simmel, Georg. 1950. "The Stranger." In *The Sociology of Georg Simmel,* ed. K. H. Wolff. New York: Free Press. 402–408.

Simon, Stephanie. 2008. "Atheists Reach Out—Just Don't Call It Proselytizing." *Wall Street Journal,* November 18.

Smith, Christian. 1998. *American Evangelicalism: Embattled and Thriving.* Chicago: University of Chicago Press.

Smith, Christian, ed. 2003. *The Secular Revolution.* Berkeley: University of California Press.

Smith, Christopher, and Richard Cimino. 2012. "Atheisms Unbound: The Role of the New Media in the Formation of a Secularist Identity." *Secularism and Nonreligion,* 1:17–31, http://dx.doi.org/10.5334/snr.ab.

Smith, Jesse. 2011. "Becoming an Atheist in America: Constructing Identity and Meaning from the Rejection of Theism." *Sociology of Religion,* 72:2, Summer: 215–237.

Smith, Jessie. 2013. "Creating a Godless Community: The Collective Identity Work of Contemporary American Atheists." *Journal for the Scientific Study of Religion,* 52:1, March: 80–99.

Snider, Chris. 2005. "Five Questions with Sam Harris." *Eudaimonist Newsletter*, 7:1:, January: 1–3.

Speciale, Alessandro. 2013. "Pope Francis Tells Atheists to 'Obey Their Conscience.'" *Religion News Service*, September 11, http://www.religionnews.com/2013/09/11/pope-francis-tells-atheists-to-obey-their -conscience/.

Stark, Rodney. 2008. *What Americans Really Believe*. Waco, TX: Baylor University Press.

Stark, Rodney. 2012. *America's Blessings: How Religion Benefits Everyone, Including Atheists*. West Conshohocken, PA: Templeton Press.

Stark, Rodney, and Roger Finke. 2000. *Acts of Faith*. Princeton, NJ: Princeton University Press.

Streib, Heinz, and Constantin Klein. 2012. "Atheists, Agnostics, and Apostates." In *APA Handbook of Psychology, Religion, and Spirituality*, ed. Kenneth Pargament. 713–728. Washington, DC: APA Books.

Tabash, Edward. 2004. "Atheism Is Indeed a Civil Rights Issue: Struggling for Equality Before the Law." *Free Inquiry*, 24:4, June–July: 44.

Taira, Teemu. 2012. "New Atheism as Identity Politics." In *Religion and Knowledge: Sociological Perspectives*, ed. Matthew Guest and Elisabeth Arweck. Farnham, UK: Ashgate. 31-43.

Taylor, Charles. 2002. *Varieties of Religion Today: William James Revisited*. Cambridge, MA: Harvard University Press.

Taylor, Charles. 2007. *A Secular Age*. Cambridge, MA: Harvard University Press.

Taylor, Keith. 2006. "Atheists in Cyberspace." *Free Inquiry*, 26:1, December/January: 51–52.

Torpy, Jason. 2013. "Army of God: America's Armed Forces vs. Their Nontheists." *Free Inquiry*, 33:3, April/May: 20–21.

vjack. 2011. "When Mockery Is Effective." *Atheist Revolution*, http://www.atheistrev.com/2011/03/when-mockery-is-effective.html.

Wallace, Anthony F. C. 1970. *Culture and Personality*. New York: Random House.

Walter, Nicholas. 1998. *Humanism*. Amherst, NY: Prometheus Books.

Warren, Sidney. 1966. *American Freethought*. New York: Gordian Press.

Williamson, David A., and George Yancey. 2013. *There Is No God: Atheists in America*. Lanham, MD: Rowman and Littlefield.

Wilson, Bryan. 1982. *Religion in Sociological Perspective*. Oxford: Oxford University Press.

Wilson, Jane. 1990. *Funerals Without God*. Buffalo, NY: Prometheus Books.

Winston, Kimberly. 2012. "Do Atheists Have a Sexual Harassment Problem?" *Religion News Service*, July 12, http://articles.washingtonpost.com/2012-07-12/national/35486345_1_sexual-harassment-sexual-attention-skeptic.

Winston, Kimberly. 2013. "Atheists, the Next Generation: Unbelief Moves Further into the Mainstream." *Publishers' Weekly*, April 12, http://www.publishersweekly.com/pw/by-topic/industry-news/religion/article/56789-atheists-the-next-generation-unbelief-moves-further-into-the-mainstream.html.

Zuckerman, Phil. 2007. "Atheism: Contemporary Numbers and Patterns." In *The Cambridge Companion to Atheism*, ed. Michael Martin. New York: Cambridge University Press. 47–68.

Zuckerman, Phil. 2011. *Faith No More: Why People Reject Religion.* New York: Oxford University Press.

Zuckerman, Phil, ed. 2010. *Atheism and Secularity.* Vols. 1 and 2. Santa Barbara, CA: Praeger.

ABOUT THE AUTHORS

Richard Cimino is founding editor of Religion Watch, a monthly publication reporting on trends and research in contemporary religion. He currently teaches sociology at the University of Richmond in Virginia and is the author of several books on religion, including The Most Scientific Religion, Trusting the Spirit, and co-author of Shopping for Faith.

Christopher Smith is an independent researcher. His areas of interest include secularism and social theory. He holds an M.A. in Sociology from the New School for Social Research.

INDEX